Transforming Government

Transforming Government

Performance Driven IT

Mr. Ernest Pages & Mr. Stephen Gousie

ISBN-10: 1511542977
ISBN-13: 9781511542975
Library of Congress Control Number: 2014923018
CreateSpace Independent Publishing Platform
North Charleston, South Carolina

Introduction

As LOCAL GOVERNMENT managers, we all want to use information technology (IT) that helps our governments serve the community by reducing costs, expanding services, and eliminating risk. Sometimes it's not easy. This book is intended to be a practical guide for local government managers wanting to maximize the value of IT in their organizations. It provides recommendations for aligning IT with local government's strategic vision, identifying opportunities to leverage technology, as well as tackling the ever-challenging step of getting started.

Simply adopting individual technologies to fulfill each need as it arises is not the answer. This short-sighted approach has helped to install many of the incompatible technologies that live within our local governments today. We must approach technology from the broader perspective as facilitator of an integrated organization that works together. As our governments adopt more complex technologies, we need quality management systems to ensure that we are aligned – and not in conflict – with the goals of our business.

If problems exist within the IT infrastructure, there are a whole host of headaches and issues that can slow or even stop government services. Nevertheless, we have seen that if IT is set up and managed properly, it can help local government managers <u>save taxpayer dollars</u>, <u>reduce business risk</u>, <u>enhance services</u> delivered to the community, and possibly even <u>identify new revenue streams</u>. Most of us are looking to get the job done without breaking the bank.

Local governments are in the process of a metamorphosis. Our organizations are transitioning from a collection of isolated departments with separate functions and deliverables, to a unified business that shares information through linked processes.

Along with this spirit of transformation, we must be able to use our IT resources more wisely. Communities are increasing their demands for services, while challenging economic times are intensifying downward fiscal pressures. As a result, local governments are searching for ways to lower their cost to serve – examining both what services are provided and how they are delivered. Changing political leadership and evolving technologies can often make achieving effective IT seem impossible.

At the core, it is important to understand industry norms and how your IT group compares in terms of functionality, structure and cost to other successful government IT organizations. Having personally weathered the storm and realigned technology to enable – and not inhibit – our ability to serve the community, I can assure you that with a little clear thinking and the right team you can transform your government.

– Cindy Johnson, ICMA-CM, City Manager, Richland, Washington

Table of Contents

1

What's Wrong with IT Anyway?

N O ONE DISAGREES that the IT department in local government is operating in a challenging environment. They are expected to improve customer service, provide 24/7 support, and deliver non-stop continuity of IT operations. At the same time, they are facing leaner budgets, fundamental shifts in how information is organized through geographic-based systems (GIS), and restructuring of how the data center functions through virtualization and the cloud...and did we mention improve customer service?

Very few people understand what IT does and why IT costs so much. It is often considered a cost center and a back-office necessity; and at its worst, a group of people who says, "No!" first and asks questions later. They often have the reputation of being defensive, late, overpriced, uninformed and unhelpful.

Despite these challenges, other organizations have been able to overcome the negative perceptions and deliver successful IT services. So we have to ask ourselves... *what's wrong with local government IT anyway?*

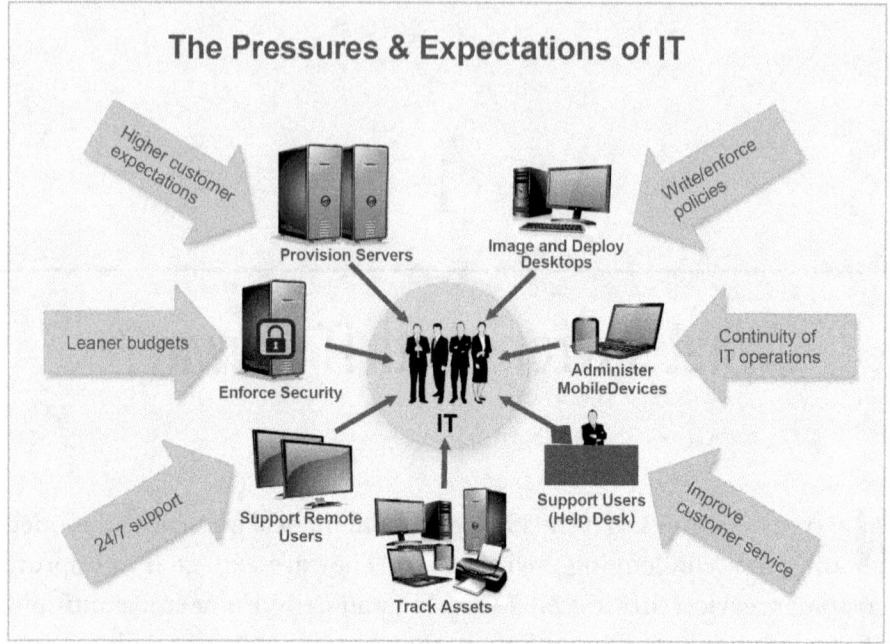

Figure 1-1 The pressures and expectations of IT

GETTING A CLEAR VIEW

There are certainly a number of fundamental problems faced by local government IT. We're going to focus on the biggest and most troublesome ones.

The most significant problem is rooted in how technology has been deployed. Historically, the departments within local governments have operated as independent silos. There was limited inter-departmental collaboration, so this arrangement seemed natural. Each department went about its business and, over the years, adopted technologies to fulfill their own needs. The IT department's role was to just make each department's technology choices work and ask no questions. IT knew very little about departmental goals, and as expected, had little involvement in the selection process.

Of course, that left the departments making technology investment decisions. Typically, they knew little about technology and made decisions based on what looked best, which company had the best salesperson, or what came recommended from someone they knew. The technology fit – whether it would work for their department or was compatible with the City's other systems was not considered. Once committed to a strategic direction, managers then had to focus their energy on getting such a major investment funded.

It may seem obvious, but many people forget that if an IT project does not ultimately support business goals, it should not be pursued. There are times when technologies get approved and funded based on how vocal or well-connected the sponsors are – not necessarily based on the value of the technology to the overall organization. Those situations are sometimes the toughest to fix because a small fortune was spent deploying the technologies, and management does not want to admit they made a mistake. They want to believe that there *must* be a way to salvage it.

We end up with a hodge-podge of technologies that the IT department must cobble together. In one case, an agency was running multiple strategic systems (e.g., desktop operating system, user authentication, network operating system, email, and mainframe applications) each from different vendor architectures. The lack of coordination among these systems drained IT resources dramatically since IT had to develop workarounds to enable the disparate systems to operate. This complexity within the core systems had been made even more difficult by the introduction of mostly unsecure, consumer-grade mobile devices (e.g., smartphones, tablets) into the enterprise.

Beyond the aggravating interruptions in service caused by incompatible technologies, IT is not able to respond quickly to changing conditions. Departments look at service interruptions as IT's failure when it's often caused by the conflicting departmental IT systems. Ultimately, senior management must entrust the organization's technology to IT. In turn, IT must take ownership of the technology environment, understand how it fits into the business environment, and provide the leadership needed to create order.

The siloed view of business processes and technology remains pervasive in local government, which limits organizational effectiveness and efficiency. *So how do we connect these silos and begin operating as a unified government? What role can IT play in building the bridge?*

It's time that we all took a step back and looked candidly at the technologies and processes used within our governments. Getting an honest view of the situation is essential for defining an effective role for technology and IT management. Look beyond the task alone and think about the business processes that reach across those functional areas. At the end of the day, we're looking to keep local government operating on a limited budget without interruption.

The processes we use today – day in and day out – were developed years or even decades ago. Systems were implemented to strictly automate processes that may not even be necessary today. Before we go through the expense of automation, it's important to analyze the process itself to: 1) understand how it operates across functions; and 2) look for ways to streamline it.

In many cases, there are procedures running end-to-end across departmental lines that can be simplified and combined. This is a business operations issue, not strictly an IT issue. Merging inefficient processes can help to eliminate redundant work, cut costs, and accelerate your city's response time.

TRANSFORMING THE ROLE OF IT

Local governments are experiencing their own e-government transformation. Greater demand is being placed on just-in-time (JIT) information and services in what many are calling the "Amazon-ization" of local government.

Amazon-ization means that customers want more than basic information on local government websites. They want transactional websites that can accept and process applications, requests, payments, and generally improve two-way communication.

In addition the explosive use of social media, cloud-based services and mobility has created a society with "no-wait" service expectations. Users now expect the same level of simplicity when accessing government systems as they do from any large company or retailer. IT is being asked to respond to these trends while still maintaining existing inefficient operations.

To accomplish this transformation, governments must rethink every aspect of how they provide services to citizens. If you're prepared, and the planning and execution are handled properly, your government could start solving problems quicker and improving services to the community.

In the end, the potential of IT is not being maximized if it is viewed solely as a resource that maintains the network and computers. IT is a powerful strategic tool to government that needs to be utilized as such. Organizations that have empowered IT to be a strategic enabler and internal consultant have reaped the rewards of a high performing government.

Are you ready to start?

THERE IS HOPE

By using technology intelligently, many local governments are capable of improving the delivery of existing services and even expanding their services for the same, or even less, investment over time. For example, local governments are able to offer residents access to information 24 hours a day/7 days a week/365 days a year, and launch online transactions that integrate directly into government systems requiring little support from staff. *Too good to be true?* It's not.

In any case, if you're reading this book, chances are you've reached the point where you are ready to transform your government and create an IT function that delivers value.

Recognizing there is a problem is the first step to correcting it. Every local government manager does not need to become an authority on IT to make IT work for their government. This book is intended to serve as a practical guide to help you improve the effectiveness of your IT organization. Once you understand the issues you are facing, you are better equipped to apply some clear thinking and achieve the results you want.

Consider these questions as they relate to your government:

- *Does IT contribute strategically to your operations? How?*
- *How efficient are your processes across departments?*
- *Does your organization operate mostly on paper based forms and approvals?*
- *Does your governing body want to offer greater access to government services to citizens? Are those needs being met?*
- *Does IT assist with ideas on how to help bridge the gap between improved service needs and reduced budgets?*
- *Is IT your trusted technology advisor?*

2

The First Step: What Problem?

THE EFFECTIVENESS OF it is typically measured by the quality of service provided. You may be asking yourself: *What are the warning signs of a problem with IT?* It begins with management having little or no idea of what IT is doing or why. As a result, IT can become overloaded with too much to do, and no way to catch up.

It's obvious when support requests take a week or more to be resolved, and there is a serious backlog of technology projects. Inefficient IT environments consider delays normal; and many times IT projects waffle between being active, to on-hold, then back again to active. Many times these projects never get done at all. In the end, IT is unable to provide help desk callers with effective support, and users do not want to use IT and attempt to bypass IT for support services.

MANAGING PRIORITIES

Assuming the IT organization is staffed within standard levels for local government, your IT team should not need to work a lot of overtime to complete projects. Excessive overtime is an indication that IT is overcommitted with too many projects and too many support calls, which puts the quality of work and transformation at risk. In response, management typically approves overtime or adds staff, which may help reduce the backlog temporarily, but the backlog soon returns when processes return to normal. *How can you end this reactive IT management cycle?*

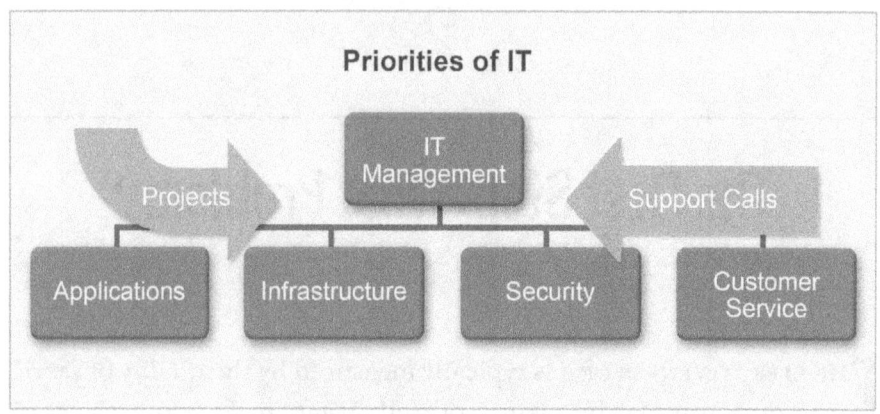

Figure 2-1 The priorities of IT

Projects and support calls need to be managed closely to avoid reactive and inefficient responses. Well-planned and prioritized projects ensure that expectations across the entire organization, and especially for the IT team, are clear and actionable.

If excessive workloads are not controlled, IT staff can experience early burn-out, which results in low morale and high turnover. This type of inconsistent workload can negatively affect the IT infrastructure, too. The framework can become fragmented since so many people – with different perspectives and priorities – have maintained the system.

Who sets the scope of projects and priorities for IT? Does it really matter? Absolutely. According to the Information Technology Process Institute, an independent research organization, only 29% of all IT projects are successfully completed on time, within budget, and with all of the required features and functions.[1] When asked why their projects were

---

1 Source: CHAOS 2012 Third Quarter Research Report, The Standish Group International

challenged, 50% of the rework was attributed to issues with the initial scope of requirements. IT was doing what it was requested instead of asking its customers the right questions to define the scope correctly from the start. *Why not?* Respondents said it would take too much time. *Ironic, isn't it?*

Finally, 18% of IT projects were cancelled prior to completion or delivered and never used. Of those failures, 70% were due to poor project scoping requirements. This research illustrates exactly what any experienced project manager knows – thorough planning of priorities and project scope is essential for a successfully completed project.

Another sign of problems within your IT department is when unplanned downtime (i.e., when computers or the network stop working) is viewed as an unavoidable part of normal business. This does not have to be a part of your operations.

Although technologies are not always fail-proof, it is now standard practice to establish backup or "failover" processes. Technologies exist to support IT services if the primary systems fail. Our work has shown that many IT organizations spend nearly half of their time on unplanned or unscheduled work or "firefighting."

By contrast, research indicates that high performing IT organizations spend less than 5% of their time dealing with unplanned downtime[2]. Although in our experience, organizations investing less than 25% of their time dealing with downtime tend to be fairly stable.

Who's in Charge

The organization may have a problem if the individual managing IT does not understand, nor can explain, the total cost of IT services, infrastructure and projects. Just because it's technical does not mean it shouldn't have a good business justification. It's baffling when management does not have the same business expectations for their IT department as other departments.

---

2 Source: Information Technology Process Institute

To be a contributor at a strategic level requires leadership – just like any other department. IT is not just about deploying and maintaining the network and computers. Talented IT management can provide direction, both strategic and tactical, that improves the productivity and cost-effectiveness of the entire organization.

There's a basic flaw in how senior management selects an IT manager. Typically, they find a smart "techie" to lead the IT team. This individual's strength is understanding technology, but not necessarily how it relates to operating a business. Even worse, this person may not be very skilled at explaining the value of new technologies to management, or managing expectations – even their own – for projects.

To further complicate the issue, this technophile then hires an entire IT team that thinks and communicates exactly like him or her. Management assumes the IT manager knows what they are talking about since they spew technical lingo and acronyms, but everyone forgets to ask how any of the projects will advance the business of the organization.

Senior management would never consider glossing over the details of the budget or a financial report. They would be very clear on all of the reported numbers and what it means to their government. It's time to take IT seriously and run it as professionally as any other function of local government.

The responsibility ultimately lies with management needing to understand the true scope of the job, hire the right people – both employees and vendors – and treat the IT department like a business function. Many times management does not understand the IT function, and trusts that IT is running smoothly. When performance declines, they don't know where to turn, which is a risky situation for the health of the entire organization.

The person managing IT may be well-intentioned, but if they cannot grow beyond maintaining a basic IT infrastructure to serve in a true management capacity, it's time to find someone who can. It's important to find IT managers with the leadership, knowledge and experience for managing an organization. People managing IT require a strong understanding of business strategy, leadership and technology. It is also important that they are able to serve and guide their customers.

With the right person in an IT leadership role, technology projects have a better chance of being aligned with the organization's strategic business objectives. Open communication ensures that IT has what it needs to support the vision. Quite simply, it is a new way of thinking about IT. It requires active involvement by the departmental customers to work with IT in a way that ensures ongoing alignment with business priorities.

As IT becomes more strategic to the organization, the IT manager becomes more involved in visionary planning and manages relationships more than operations. IT needs to be viewed as an agile, on-demand service that creates value for the organization. IT service management becomes an indispensable function equipped with relationship management and high level communication skills.

Consider these questions as they relate to your government:

- *How are IT priorities managed?*
- *How much of your IT department's work is planned vs. unplanned?*
- *Is there a list of backlogged IT projects?*
- *Are there unexpected outages of your network?*
- *Is there high turnover in your IT department?*
- *Is your IT organization skilled at project management?*

3

Business-Driven Technology Strategy

A S DISCUSSED EARLIER, there has been a shift in how work is performed within local governments over the last two decades. Instead of focusing on work automation to improve efficiency, IT systems are now capable of delivering the information that managers need to make the right decisions at the right time, which improves business effectiveness. With increasingly tight budgets, organizations reduce costs by improving efficiency, effectiveness and becoming more technologically advanced.

To respond to these challenges, IT must become an innovation partner to help transform the business. Complex and costly projects, such as ERP, Police, Court or Public Works online applications, must be shown as sound investments.

Developing an IT strategy that supports the government business strategy is essential for a productive and effective IT department. Without a clear and defined IT strategy, the contributions of IT will be random and inconsistent, and fail to meet customers' expectations and needs. We can all agree that a straightforward IT strategy keeps the IT team focused on common objectives, and controls the expectations of the rest of the organization.

So it stands to reason that it would be a waste of time and energy to create an IT strategy without having a business strategy in place for your local government. Clearly determining the goals and direction of the entire organization is required before you begin defining an IT strategy with departmental objectives and tactics.

We've witnessed many IT managers struggling to create a plan that everyone supports. *Why are they struggling?* Because the business strategy is incomplete or lacking clarity. Trying to design a strategy for a department, when the entire organization isn't clear on their goals and direction, is nearly impossible.

It's a strange balancing act. You cannot create an IT strategy without a business strategy, but conversely IT can also contribute to the direction of the business strategy. IT management can offer valuable insight into what is possible and how business objectives can be achieved because they see the organization at its most fundamental level. They see how information flows throughout the organization and how business processes cross departmental silos to connect the whole organization.

IT management can fill a vital role in identifying and designing new cross-departmental processes, determining accurate metrics, as well as defining the scope of responsibility for the new IT organization. They are uniquely qualified to recommend leading technologies that can solve problems and improve operations.

Beyond simply aligning IT with the business, IT must also serve as a strategic contributor, and avoid being viewed as simply an expensive tactical cost center that can be outsourced easily.

TRANSFORMATIONAL ROADMAP

Over the last 20 years, investing in IT has been focused on daily operations without considering the bigger picture. PCs were bought to improve productivity, and networks were created to improve communication. With the introduction of digital government, the motivations for investing in technology and the role of IT have been changing.

IT departments have traditionally been seen as a support function. To effectively undergo the transformation to digital government, IT should ideally be viewed as an equal partner to the functional, citizen-facing departments. The quality of service provided by the local government to the community is dependent upon recasting the IT department in a greater role.

Technology serves an important function in every department's business processes. IT still must support core business functions, while also leading core cross-departmental information management and technology functions.

The digital government transformation focuses on information *management* more than information *technology*. Emphasis is better placed on the organization and control of the structure, processing and delivery of information – not simply software and hardware. As such, management will ensure that technology investments are determined by clearly defined business requirements.

Technology is a powerful tool for improving the integration of each department's information flow to meet the city's strategic direction and better serve the community. Ultimately, more efficient collaborative planning and coordination of projects, resources and funding will accelerate the city's goals and objectives.

THE PROMISE OF DIGITAL GOVERNMENT

With the widespread adoption of the Internet and e-commerce, governments at all levels realize the same technologies present an opportunity to deliver information and services more efficiently.

The idea of a "digital government" promises effective, reliable and secure electronic access to government 24 hours a day, 7 days a week, 365 days a year. Residents and businesses may access online resources for information about government services, conduct business or personal transactions, or participate in improvement efforts. Services and information may be accessed through traditional service channels, such as mail, telephone or in-person at a local government facility; or people may prefer the Internet, email or social media.

Digital government also promises to untether staff from their desks, allowing them to perform complex operations instantly wherever they are. Currently, staff may have to return to the office to input or synchronize the data they have collected, or use unreliable or intermittent connectivity from the field. Imagine the productivity gains from applications written for work performance in the field that can operate in low bandwidth environments. This flexibility improves both workflow, staff productivity, as well as morale.

In addition, digital government promises to help local government management with easy-to-read, targeted performance management tools, such as dashboards and balanced scorecards. Gone are the days of month-end reports that managers comb through to determine their performance weeks ago. Digital government promises information on managers' desktops reporting information that is pertinent to each individual doing their job – now in real-time. The time between data collection, analysis and decision-making is now reduced from weeks to minutes.

Local governments are under constant budget pressure. Digital government promises to lessen the demands on traditional service channels like telephone, mail and in-person, enabling cities to shift resources from outdated service channels to new services channels that accelerate information sharing and response times. Best of all, overall service will improve for residents. Planned, prudent investment in technology enables residents to conduct transactions with minimal local government staff involvement, and helps to soften the effects of growing demands from a swelling population on the government staff.

Though digital government holds many promises, government organizations are also required to enhance customer service and demonstrate fiscal restraint. Expectations of effective customer service and access to services have fundamentally changed with Internet use. Citizens expect information to be available on-demand, and services to be accessed whenever and wherever. Municipalities are expected to meet these standards in order to maintain citizens' satisfaction levels.

3 PHASES OF DIGITAL GOVERNMENT

Fulfilling the promises of a local digital government can be realized in three phases:

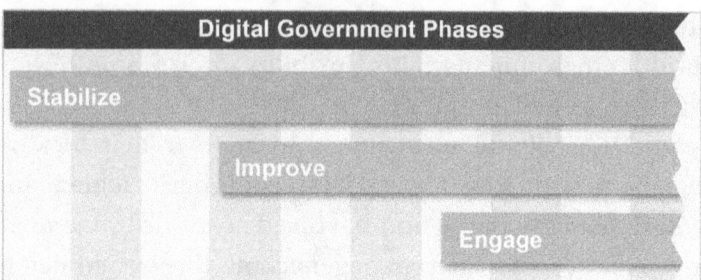

Figure 3-1 Digital government phases

PHASE 1 - STABILIZE

Much like constructing a building, transforming to digital government requires building a stable, solid foundation. A standardized and simplified network, data center, and disaster recovery processes must be capable of supporting the transaction volume, storage and security requirements, and stress that will be placed on it. The focus is on physical locations, structures, wires and switches, security provisions, and backup and disaster recovery capabilities.

PHASE 2 - IMPROVE

With a stable infrastructure in place, our attention turns to the applications or enterprise software systems that support the day-to-day operations of the organization. These applications must be robust enough to handle the organization's transaction volumes, and integrated to minimize data re-entry between component systems. In addition, these applications should have a flexible, real-time reporting capability that allows for dashboard or portal views into information needed by managers to make time-sensitive decisions.

PHASE 3 - ENGAGE

With a stable infrastructure and backend applications in place, the focus shifts to extending the local government applications through online and mobility systems. Once the applications are implemented in Phase 2, it's time to train user staff, untethering them from desktops and enabling field transactions in real-time. Residents and businesses will also need to be notified that Web-based services are available on a 24x7x365 basis.

Each phase brings its own set of challenges. Most local governments have limited resources to dedicate to creating a digital government environment, and they want to minimize the disruption to municipal operations. For these organizations, the digital government vision evolves over many years. To be accomplished effectively, however, a clear strategy must be developed and pursued.

Although presented as three distinct phases, some organizations blur the lines, pursuing multiple phases simultaneously. This approach can spell disaster by costing more money, delaying the deployment, and causing disruption to government operations. Creating a digital government requires each phase to be well-established and maintained before launching the next phase because each phase serves as the basis for the next phase.

For example, applications require a fast, reliable network. Web services running on legacy applications will run slowly and frustrate citizens instead of exciting them about the local government's new capabilities.

Varying views have emerged regarding the goals of digital government. Some believe that IT is a means for fundamentally reshaping government and democracy. Others focus more on short-term opportunities of simply enhancing the services delivered to citizens (G2C), facilitating enhanced interactions between government and businesses (G2B), as well as enhancing government operations (G2G).

Most believe that digital government helps to engage and inform the community by creating a more responsive, efficient and accountable government. Greater government accountability pressures the operating departments to deliver higher quality services on par with accepted business practices.

In the end, we can all agree that the primary goals for digital government are to satisfy customer service expectations, and increase the efficiency and effectiveness of government operations. Additionally, digital government is expected to provide access to information and transactions online, increase community participation in government, and demonstrate full disclosure and trustworthiness.

EXECUTING A DIGITAL GOVERNMENT VISION

Although the most obvious demonstrations of digital government may be improving the accessibility of government services to citizens, the digital government vision also extends to internal operations. Across the political spectrum, it is believed that the appropriate use of IT provides a basis for more effective government programs, more efficient work within government agencies, and lower total program costs. Important IT applications include reducing redundant information, enhancing government workers' access to information, and improving workflow management.

A ground up restructuring of IT departments is required to meet the challenges of a digital government transformation. It's essential for IT to adjust how it performs its work, and how it communicates and services other departments. The transformation for IT departments begins with being externally, customer-focused instead of internally, cost-focused.

Under a digital government vision, an effective IT Strategic Plan should define the baseline situation, set a direction, and identify the steps required to achieve the goals.

DEFINE THE BASELINE

Where is the IT function today? Any effective plan must start from a baseline. An unbiased analysis of the strengths and weaknesses (internal focus), and opportunities and threats (external focus) for the IT department must be conducted. This analysis should not be limited to the technology; it should include the entire organization, its structure and its processes.

SET THE DIRECTION

Where is IT going? Using the local government overall strategic and departmental plans for guidance and candid input from departments and users, the IT department establishes a clear understanding of how IT can be used to achieve organizational and departmental goals.

This strategic direction examines critical business factors including: 1) how services will be delivered to external customers (e.g., residents, citizens, businesses and visitors); and 2) how departments providing services to external customers will be supported through technology and technology-related services.

Define the charter of the IT department, specifically IT's role in leading technology innovation, and formulating, monitoring or enforcing technology-related policy, standards, protocols and purchasing. A local government IT Governance Committee (p. 22) may also be included as part of the scope to help the IT department manage its often conflicting priorities.

CLOSE THE GAP

How will IT close the gap between where it is and where it's going? In the context of the technology strategic direction and its charter, describe three to five strategic goals for the IT department to achieve by the end of each planning period. This practice will help close the gap and achieve a digital government vision.

For each of these goals, identify three to seven key projects that the IT team will do to support each goal. Finally, determine how the IT department will allocate resources during the planning period to achieve the goals and complete the projects.

Consider these questions as they relate to your government:

- *Do we have an overall business strategic plan?*
- *Is IT included in the development of the business strategic plan?*
- *Does IT provide leadership in proposing technology innovations to support the business mission?*
- *Does IT follow a strategic technology plan for evolving to digital government?*
- *What goals are reasonable for us to pursue over the next five years?*
- *What projects will advance these goals?*

4

A Model for Advancing IT

M OST IT ORGANIZATIONS today suffer from an identity crisis. In a sense, they don't know who they want to be when they grow up. Their organization has been insourced, outsourced, reorganized, centralized and decentralized – but nothing has worked. Nobody knows what to do with IT, but they know that things could be better. *What is the most effective approach to integrating IT into an organization?*

The lack of clarity on IT's role in local government has created an environment of distrust between IT and their customers, a.k.a. the departments. In some instances, IT doesn't treat their customers very well, and conversely the customers don't respect the job IT is doing.

Many times, the departments don't appreciate the scope of IT's responsibilities, don't understand the value of the money spent on IT, and are generally unsatisfied with the service they receive. Management continues to throw money at IT in an attempt to resolve problems that never seem to be fixed. They have hired CIOs, CTOs and technology gurus of every walk of life, but the investments in time and money have made little improvement in either the overall effectiveness or credibility of IT.

One familiar example is the Y2K "crisis." Enormous sums of money were spent to avoid the disastrous disruptions predicted around the Y2K transition to the new millennium. When few computer meltdowns occurred, management began to question the reality of the threat and the value of the preparation effort. Even if Y2K preparation efforts had failed, would their organizations have really faced any serious consequences?

This "Chicken Little" attitude of over-reacting to the slightest risk has prompted management to question IT's value and the judgment of IT leadership, and to wonder if IT has become simply a tool rather than an advantage.[3]

So we ask ourselves: *If we are committed to improving the performance of IT, how can the problems continue to happen?* The problem with the perceived value of IT is often the result of poor communication between management and what some have come to think of as the black hole of IT.

ASSESSING YOUR IT FUNCTION

From our perspective, the best way to start is by exploring the elements of the Clear Thinking Model as they relate to your organization. There are five basic elements for assessing your IT department that include Strategy, Governance, Architecture, Organization and Processes. The Clear Thinking Model will help you to understand in a very straightforward way, the current state of your IT organization and highlight what needs attention to improve its performance.

Clear Thinking Model
Clear Strategy
A clear technology strategy is essential for government managers to understand the business rationale for technology, how and why technology is used, as well as for future planning. Consider how IT supports the organizational strategy.

Clear Governance
A Governance Committee comprised of members of the management team is better positioned to assess the value and

---

3 "IT Doesn't Matter," Nicolas Carr, Harvard Business Review, May 2003

risk of proposed IT initiatives for the entire organization. They can set overall priorities for the IT department with a broader, integrated perspective. Proper governance prevents the IT department from becoming overwhelmed by conflicting requests.

Clear Architecture
Leverage standardized, off-the-shelf solutions to keep costs down. Technology for the sake of technology fails. The key is to deploy effective technologies to solve real problems in your government.

Clear Organization
Create an organizational structure that works. Define the role of the IT department, and the services they need to provide a smooth running organization. The right people will have the skills and knowledge, as well as a proactive attitude to resolve problems.

Clear Processes
Implementing quality management practices keeps the work process-dependent, not people-dependent. Processes that are optimized ensure that the organization is running as efficiently as possible.

STRATEGY SETS THE COURSE
Strategy means many different things to people, but for our purposes it's a plan for achieving an end result. The plan includes the tactics, or the steps, you will take to achieve that end result. Organizational change starts with the business strategic plan: rethinking the business model, rethinking business processes, re-training users, updating job scopes and requirements, and changing the rewards system.

From an IT perspective, it is important to align the IT strategy with the overall business strategy to deliver true business value.

In local government, the IT plan should help customers accomplish their goals, and it should not get bogged down in too much "techie" detail. Simply identify

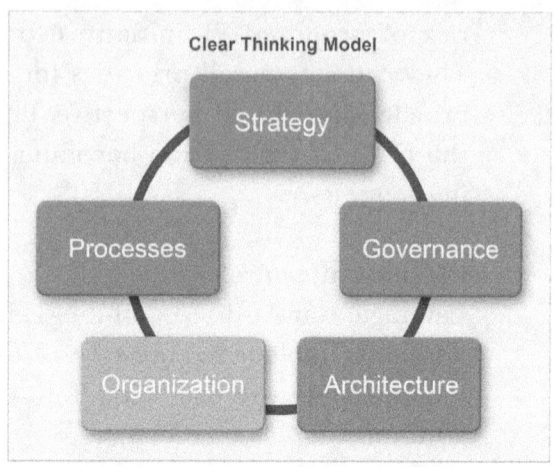

Figure 4-1 - The Clear Thinking Model

the needed services and the value to your customers, and the steps needed to achieve them. Making the strategy too complicated can stop a plan cold in its tracks. Keep it simple and straightforward to make it easy for everyone to understand and support.

An often underestimated step in strategy development is *communicating* the strategy. After taking the time to analyze and create a comprehensive plan, make sure it is easily understood by all personnel in IT, as well as the entire organization. By taking the final step of thoroughly communicating the IT plan to the entire organization, everyone will understand the objectives clearly and will be better able to support the IT plan.

Ultimately, defining an IT strategy also controls random requests from distracting the IT team from their primary objectives. If everyone is clear what the goals are and what the plan is for achieving them, there is little room for projects and ideas that do not support that common plan.

COLLABORATION DRIVES SUCCESS

Problem

In one example, a City was dealing with a multitude of projects with no clear direction on how to complete them. IT management was being pressured by local government management to produce clear timelines for project deliverables. This situation caused IT management to become indecisive and insular, ignoring users and pressuring key IT staff to affect changes. The staff morale dropped. Key staff threatened to resign and users were looking externally to implement IT systems.

Plan of Action

As part of an overall reorganization, a Governance Committee was put in place that utilized a project review and prioritization process incorporating all key department users and senior management.

Results

Projects, including the build-out of a new data center, WAN (wide area network), and modernization of GIS were completed by the existing staff on-time and on-budget without staff turnover.

GOVERNANCE CONTROLS ACTIVITIES

In many government agencies, departments will approach IT individually to request support on special projects. This practice requires the IT manager to become the gatekeeper, juggling far too many projects for a limited pool of resources, and peacemaker when projects aren't completed on time. Because each department lacks awareness of the broad range of IT projects, they become frustrated when their projects are not completed in what they consider sufficient time.

Establishing a Governance Committee removes pressure from IT managers to determine IT priorities. Comprised of senior managers – including both externally-facing departments such as Planning, Public Works, Parks, Police and Fire, and internally-facing departments such as Human Resources and Finance – a Governance Committee considers the big picture and sets IT priorities as they relate to business priorities. This Governance Committee has the citywide perspective to evaluate the risk and business value of proposed IT projects, to set the direction for IT, and to ensure that IT investments are aligned with the overall strategy.

A Governance Committee is also able to measure the effectiveness of city-wide processes. With this cross-departmental team guiding IT, better integration of core applications can be achieved. Working together on a Governance Committee will even help department heads identify ways to improve processes between their organizations and to examine where technologies purchased for one department can be leveraged across multiple departments.

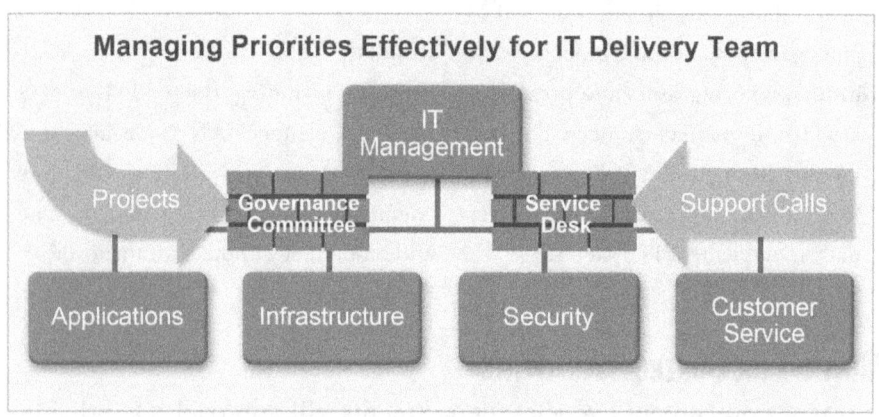

Figure 4-2 Managing priorities effectively for IT delivery team

With this layer of guidance and oversight, IT's role is not to set IT priorities, but instead focus on executing the priorities selected by the Governance Committee. In our experience, if IT priorities are determined by the managers of departments that consume 80% of IT's resources, the IT team will be able to satisfy the majority of its customers' expectations. Instead of criticizing the effectiveness of IT, the executives will understand the challenges of IT and become its greatest advocates.

ARCHITECTURE SAVES MONEY
Technology is everywhere these days, and it does not have to be complicated or the "latest and greatest" to be effective for your organization.

In many cases, tried and true systems are the wiser choice for local governments.

Adopting technology standards can make the delivery of effective technologies easier to deploy and maintain. From our perspective, simple and easy translates into cost savings for a few reasons. First, the equipment is typically widely available and priced lower. Second, these technologies have probably been available for some time, which means that they have been used and improved to the point where the bugs have been worked out and they are more reliable. Third, it doesn't require specialized (i.e., expensive) consultants to deploy, support and troubleshoot. Keeping the technology architecture simple keeps more money in your budget for other services that directly benefit the community.

Standardizing platforms and applications will also drive down costs and improve the simplicity of managing the architecture. Reduce the number of vendors involved IT, and the internal IT team will be able to support standard systems without ongoing specialized training or the support of external consultants.

Focus on infrastructure management technology that supports and integrates with key processes, making those processes more efficient. Not only does it save staff time, but you'll be purchasing fewer applications to support more functions.

There should also be special focus on eliminating unplanned work. From an architecture perspective, the goal is to conserve IT resources by *preventing* IT problems rather than *fixing* them. New technologies can adapt easily to changing processes or measurements in your environment, and automatically capture key metrics.

The IT industry is evolving through a generational change. Virtualization, cloud computing, and mobility technologies are disruptive in nature and lead to dramatic architectural changes. Traditional systems integration vendors are either experiencing the same feeling of technology overload, or have abandoned the systems integration business altogether. This combination can be paralyzing to IT management since they may find themselves unable to make an informed decision.

In this environment, the IT manager must be able to carefully orchestrate internal and external resources. Research the local market for niche vendors that provide implementation support for potential technology solutions, and allow the internal IT staff to test these promising technologies with the external vendor in order to create a "proof of concept."

Since senior management typically does not understand the process of testing new technologies, IT managers need to provide a clear explanation of the value, features and benefits as they relate to the overall strategy.

Organization Sets Expectations

You may develop a brilliant strategy complete with the perfect technologies and processes; but without leadership and an organization that strives for improvement, the plan will still fail to meet expectations. Any IT investment is meaningless if the people using the new systems don't want to change and force the new system to do things the "old way." Successful IT organizations make the effort to foster a culture of performance.

Strong leaders can proactively change viewpoints and work ethics. When management communicates the vision and creates incentives – like bonuses, comp time and recognition – and provides required training, the teams begin to take ownership of their role in government and pride in the quality of their work.

At the core of a performance culture is staff that is willing and able to take a proactive attitude toward business objectives. If the staff is apathetic and waits to be told what to do, the entire organization slows to the pace of the unmotivated individuals. Local government is a fast-paced environment that requires flexible, smart and proactive contributors. Set an example by emphasizing the importance of an organization that is designed around standard processes – not around people or personalities.

A performance culture also demands collaboration between government functions. Collaborative relationships between departments help to integrate processes between IT operations and IT security, and help to create a smooth working relationship between IT and the business users. When you keep your eye on the ball, you improve your chances of hitting a homerun, and IT needs to keep its eye on the business and its customers – not itself.

If the Governance Committee relieves some pressure from IT's project volume, a knowledgeable and efficient Service Desk is an equally important component of the organization that will relieve substantial pressure from IT's problem resolution and "firefighting." With the right people and proper training, strong Service Desks can handle a lot of calls and minimize the disruptions to IT staff caused by day-to-day troubleshooting. IT can then remain focused on delivering the tools and architecture that improve the productivity of the entire organization.

PROCESSES STREAMLINE WORKFLOW

All operations are built on processes that help us complete projects and fulfill customer needs. Once established, efforts should be made to continually optimize or fine-tune these processes. Too often we see processes – some good and some bad – spring up because of the "heroic" effort of one individual to solve the problem, which becomes the "new" process. Although this approach may get the job done, it is usually not a reliable or repeatable solution.

The purpose of process is to ensure that work quality is consistent – regardless of who is performing the work. In other words, processes should be function-dependent, not person-dependent. If only one person knows how to do something that may be critical to overall organizational operations, the organization is at risk. If that person leaves, the organization must start from scratch. Consistent performance, then, requires that processes – especially critical ones – are documented. Testing documentation to ensure the processes are communicated clearly and effectively is important to achieve the desired results.

In the case of IT processes, this can be as simple as documenting system administrative passwords or how to backup data on key systems. This dependency on a single person leaves the organization exposed and can result in overworking certain reliable, high performing employees to complete tasks. Clear processes establish benchmarks that gauge progress, while driving the organization toward systematic performance improvements that are measurable.

Start by getting to know your IT department, learn what works and what doesn't work. Establish priorities. *Where will you see the greatest positive impact on the productivity of the most personnel?* This will help you determine where to focus your efforts for maximum impact.

Core to this mission of advancing IT is building IT processes around a framework that can support the existing and future needs of your organization. If you attempt to piece a framework around an existing set of processes, you will create an ineffective system that experiences frequent failures.

Consider these questions as they relate to your government:

- *Does IT report directly to senior management?*
- *Is IT consulted by senior management during strategic business planning?*
- *How is the IT budget developed?*
- *Does IT get its direction from users directly, senior management or neither?*
- *Is IT consistently delivering the results your local government needs?*

5

The Ongoing Evolution of IT

S INCE ITS INCEPTION, the IT environment was defined by the new technologies that became available to solve old problems. The development of programmable hardware computers was instrumental during World War II in deciphering enemy codes. The subsequent development of software-programmable mainframe systems facilitated the growth of large enterprises by allowing large-scale data processing to support industries, such as banking and defense. The creation of personal computers realized Bill Gate's vision of "information at your fingertips" empowering users with computational capabilities. The Internet Revolution provided users with unparalleled access to data, information and knowledge, fueling one of the greatest leaps in the history of human productivity.

Each computing era has facilitated economic progress for each generation by delivering greater capabilities at a lower cost. Today, the IT industry is evolving toward even more nimble and powerful personal information delivery systems that enable user self-sufficiency.

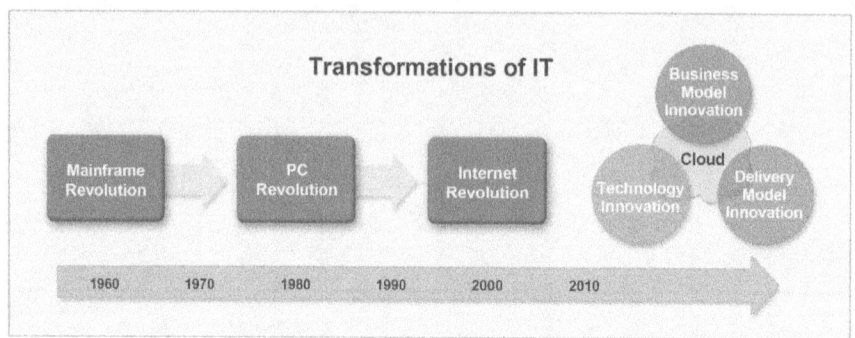

Figure 5-1 Transformations of IT

Because of this enormous change, IT departments must plan much more strategically than ever before. IT organizations must stay current with changing user needs, and the vendors transforming the industry. They must evaluate each technology as either a short-term, tactical solution or as a long-term, strategic investment. Tactical systems are projected to remain in service up to three years while there remains no predominant technology in the market. During this time, there is no way to make a certain, long-term investment. The technology market is both volatile and often unpredictable. If an IT manager is not careful, they could end up investing in the equivalent of audio compact disks (CD) rather than streaming digital media. When an approved, thoughtfully-considered, business-justified technology plan is not in place, IT may purchase technology that they consider strategic, and make substantial investments in systems that quickly become obsolete.

Poor planning can also lead to insufficient time and money invested in maintaining existing IT systems. Much like capital improvement plans that detail upgrades, improvements and maintenance for projects like roads and bridges, the IT infrastructure should also be managed as a capital investment.

In some organizations, once the IT infrastructure has been set up, it is not maintained with any consistency. Though it may not be as visible as a pothole, it doesn't take long for the system to begin showing cracks and breaking down. What you will witness is over-extended IT staff working long hours, emergency requests to replace equipment, network outages, or computers that just stop working. In short, your IT department becomes reactive, constantly firefighting, with no time for customers and their organizational improvement projects.

Organizations are particularly vulnerable to this type of situation if the IT staff has not been properly trained in maintaining the system. It can also happen if the workload is so heavy that the staff does not have the capacity to maintain the infrastructure, or there is insufficient funding to purchase upgrades or replacement parts. Industry benchmarks detail standards among equivalent sized government entities, and can help determine whether this is a real funding issue or if there are inefficiencies in the way technology resources are spent.

Introducing new technologies can greatly improve the efficiency and effectiveness of how government works. Smartphones, tablets and cloud computing fall within an evolving model in the technology world...a drive for user self-sufficiency. Since the widespread adoption of the personal computer, users have been promised more control over their processes, and easier access to the information needed to make the *right decisions at the right time*. That promise has remained largely unfulfilled. Data access still requires significant involvement by IT departments, who understand database structures and the mysterious processes needed to extract information from these systems.

Each technology can be transformative, but if implemented incorrectly can lead to substantial capital organizational costs. Some existing and evolving technologies create the greatest management challenges for IT decision makers include social media, mobility and smartphones, virtualization and cloud services.

SOCIAL MEDIA FOR CITIZEN SERVICE

The "Amazon-ization" of business, such as call centers and e-business, have raised expectations among consumers, who now require services to be available 24/7/365 via telephone, email or online. As a result, government services are now also expected to be more customer-oriented and overcome the barriers of time of day. Citizens expect to be able to perform transactions when they want, not just when government offices are open, regardless of where the customer is located.

Customer service automated phone systems and websites routinely found in the private sector are becoming more common in government. But many times there are exceptions to standard communications. Websites may provide email links to connect with a specific customer service representative for problem resolution. These capabilities are especially important for efficient, effective handling of exceptional circumstances whose resolution requires more than standard procedures.[4]

As if IT departments didn't have enough challenges, social media has surfaced as a new citizen service vehicle. Social media tools, like Facebook, Twitter and Instagram, are changing how local governments interact with residents and vice versa. Research indicates that governments are using social media to bring citizens closer to government, and facilitate an improved conversation with government.[5] Examples of the use of social media include:

- **Drive citizens to specific websites** – Some organizations use Twitter to drive users back to specific areas of their website. This

---

4 Customer satisfaction has been addressed extensively in literature on marketing (Churchill and Surprenant, 1982; Oliver and DeSarbo, 1988; Anderson and Sullivan, 1993). Although empirical evidence is limited, increases in customer satisfaction are generally believed to lower transaction costs, reduce customer turnover, lower employee turnover, enhance reputation, and reduce failure costs.

5 The Govloop Guide – Social Media Experiment in Government, Andrew Krzmarzick, 2012

allows governments to build a relationship with users, and push them toward content to take further action.

- **Reach citizens during key initiatives** – Some agencies use social media during bond referendums to highlight important information and reach people within the community who otherwise would not have paid attention to the referendum.
- **Get accurate information out more quickly during emergencies** – Some cities use Twitter to get quick information to the press and other stakeholders about emergencies, events and other issues.
- **Receive valuable data from citizens in real-time** – Governments are engaging citizens to encourage more civic activism by providing a platform for citizens to report crime, potholes, as well as building applications to improve collaboration.

The role of social media in government is still evolving. The consumer market is driving adoption, and cities must determine how they will utilize this new technology or risk being perceived as disconnected, out of touch or uncaring.

For local government, social media tools pose network and data security challenges, records retention issues, and control of who "speaks" for the organization. Research indicates that there still exists a general lack of tangible goals in the use of social media.[6] Therefore, significant change is needed in government culture, philosophy of control, and resource management before broad sustainable success can be achieved in the use of social media.

As always, IT can help facilitate in the deployment of social media support systems, however senior management must address the challenges and opportunities of social media and provide guidance to the staff. Policy needs to be set by management, and implemented by IT.

---

6 A Review of Social Media Use in E-Government, Michael J. Magro, Byrd School of Business, Shenandoah University, 1460 University Drive, Winchester, VA 2260, 2012

SMARTPHONES LEAD THE CHARGE

Revolutionary technology change came from an unexpected place… the cellular phone. Along with its affordability and easy adoption by a new generation of workers, smartphones decoupled the desktop from perhaps the most important and widely used application in the work environment – email.

Many cities perceived smartphones as expensive mobile phones, instead of inexpensive mobile computers. There were also concerns about the risks associated with smartphones – from security issues to loss of control over records retention. Blackberry® was able to close this gap for nearly a decade. However, technology-savvy workers began pushing for smartphones capabilities that Blackberry was slow to support. They brought their own, newer smartphones to work and wanted access to the network and the data on that network. Local government responded by either providing newer smartphones or allowing employees to BYOD (Bring Your Own Device).

The explosion of smartphone and tablet adoption among consumers should be approached by government organizations with caution. IT departments are facing BYOD pressures from employees of all levels, but it is a complicated issue. Before unleashing a BYOD program in your organization, be sure to understand the advantages and possible long-term drawbacks of allowing employees to use their own smartphones and tablets.

Employees want the flexibility of mobile devices with current business applications, while organizations may benefit from cost savings and productivity increases. However, additional support and management costs, and more importantly the security risk to confidential information, can far outweigh productivity gains.

What happens if a device is lost, stolen or infected with malware? Organizations have less control over personal devices, which makes sensitive data more vulnerable. IT managers cannot dictate what is acceptable on personnel's smartphones and tablets, and may lose sensitive data when employees leave an organization.

There are technology solutions to some of these challenges, but they can be very costly to implement and maintain. IT must also be trained to use them properly. The less expensive, simpler approach is to implement mobility with a policy. It is the place to start, regardless of how you proceed.

Policies regarding BYOD need to be developed and enforced, as well as strategies to manage, maintain, connect, and protect the devices. IT should be prepared for the additional strain on the corporate infrastructure from personal devices connecting to internal systems. All employees who participate in the program must fully understand and agree to the BYOD policies instituted.

IT departments need to consider workers' privacy concerns with employer access to personal information, applications and other data. It is a challenging balancing act for IT to protect the organization's sensitive data while preserving workers' rights to privacy. Ultimately, a successful BYOD program is based on a clearly defined program and an informed workforce that understands how to use their devices to conduct business without compromising security.

KEEPING UP WITH MOBILITY

This was just the beginning. The idea of mobility – the ability to get work done without being tied to one particular physical location or device, like your desktop computer – has been around for decades, but the touch-enabled smartphone was the innovation that made this a reality. Users needed more functionality, wanting what they could do on their PCs on their mobile devices; this inspired larger screens and keyboards on mobile devices.

The need for greater functionality (e.g., office applications, printing), larger screens and keyboards on mobile devices led to the evolution of tablets. Municipal applications (e.g., code enforcement, inspections, fleet) are now being written for the tablet environment. Cell phone companies have evolved their networks from 3G to 4G LTE providing near

LAN speed connections (i.e., 10 Mbs or greater) coverage in many locations. The convergence of these factors had a profound effect on the traditional desktop PC environment, which challenged the Microsoft® Windows® operating system. In response, Microsoft introduced the hybrid version of its operating system, Windows 8, which was designed to facilitate the transition from desktops to tablets.

According to the research firm, Gartner, mobility is one of the driving forces behind the $3.7 trillion that IT organizations will spend globally in 2014; mobile device sales will rise to $689 billion.[7] In addition, mobility concerns are shifting from Internet access to applications as mobile data becomes cheaper.[8] This transformation is challenging IT's ability to plan, deploy and manage the end-user environment since most of IT's staffing models and experience is based on a 20 year old technology frame of reference.

Even as tablets have become increasingly commonplace, many IT leaders still struggle with how to implement the devices at their organizations. Standard consumer applications are readily available, but tablet-based enterprise applications are not. In most cases, issuing the device itself is the easy part of a tablet deployment. Determining how to upgrade or modify the back office applications to leverage tablet technology is far more challenging and costly.

The most effective approach to providing tablet PC and touch-based applications designed for the smaller tablet form factor is to develop the applications in the native operating system of the tablet PC (e.g., iPad-iOS, Google-Android, Microsoft Windows). Another option is to develop HTML5 applications that execute most of the applications on a web server, but with a much richer application experience for the tablet PC user.

Deciding which development environment to use affects both user effectiveness and the investments needed to develop and integrate the new applications.

---

7 "Gartner Says Worldwide IT Spending on Pace to Reach $3.8 Trillion in 2014," ZDNet.com, April 2, 2014.

8 "Enterprise Software, Devices to Fuel IT Spending Growth in 2014, Gartner Says," InfoWorld, April 2, 2014.

IT INVESTMENTS CAN SAVE MONEY

The functional demands, expenses, complexity and risks of new technologies can sometimes be intimidating. When approached with clear business objectives in mind, deploying new technologies does not have to be an overwhelming task. Although requiring some investment at the front-end, costs many times are recouped quickly and lead to long-term savings.

It's much like renovating a building. It costs money to modernize it, but money is saved in future years through innovations like using more energy-efficient materials – not to mention the working environment is a lot more comfortable when it is properly arranged and outfitted.

IT is clearly challenged. The transformation of the IT industry is forcing IT organizations to transform into a sophisticated services-based organization. This transformation is not possible for IT organizations that fail to properly plan.

If your government is striving to improve the quality of customer service, and departments are looking to automate in order to reduce costs where possible, then clearly your organization should solicit IT for help. Yet, to be credible and serve as both consultant and technology leader, IT departments must be able to understand the business. This transformation requires planning, and shifting the organization from a reactive service provider to a proactive consultative organization. Many IT departments are threatened by this type of transformation because they lack the vision and/or the skills to change. But the transformation is being demanded by their customers. IT management can drive the change or fall victim to it.

Consider these questions as they relate to your government:

- *Does your IT department propose new technologies, or resist them?*
- *How are you managing the move to mobility?*
- *Are tablets and smartphones tools restricted to Council and management, or are they used by personnel working in the field?*
- *Are you restricting access to social media tools? What are your plans for managing it?*

- *Do you have clear policies in place and budgeted staffing levels to support increased citizen contact through social media?*
- *Do you budget for technology maintenance and increasing support?*
- *What are you doing with GIS? Are you simply showing maps on your website or is GIS integrated with your core applications like ERP and Police CAD?*

6

Virtualization and the Cloud

O VER THE PAST 30 years, the IT industry has been evolving, reducing the size and number of servers and distributing workstation clients (i.e., terminals) to connect to the servers over the network. The advent of more powerful servers and virtualization software has replaced this model. Virtualization introduces a new level of flexibility, performance, scalability and reliability into the IT infrastructure, and in some ways, re-invents the mainframe environment with speed and efficiency.

The move toward mobility has spawned the move toward cloud computing. With cloud computing, applications and data reside in a facility off-site that is accessible to users anytime, anywhere. Among the chief concerns with cloud computing is security and data control. More than any other aspect of the mobility change, cloud computing is a threat to the staff in traditional IT departments that provide technology infrastructure, since most of the traditional infrastructure support provided by IT can be outsourced.

With IT resources provided as an outsourced, cloud-based service, organizations no longer need substantial onsite IT support. While there is much less control of the IT infrastructure, the benefit is lower capital investments in server hardware and other overhead costs, as well as more flexibility to raise and lower capacity as needed. In addition, it frees up IT staffing to shift from server administration to the under-served areas of network administration, security, business analysis, and project management.

INTRO TO SERVER VIRTUALIZATION

Virtualization is used to condense system footprints and improve resource utilization by running several software-based computers, called virtual machines (VM), simultaneously on a single physical server computer. Each VM is a duplicate copy of an entire physical comput-ing environment. A single physical computer can simultaneously host several VMs, each running a different operating system and variety of applications. VMs on the host computer are managed by a hypervisor or Virtual Machine Manager (VMM). The VMM also manages the physical computing resources, and dynamically allocates resources to each VM as they are needed.

Most organizations adopt virtualization for lower system infra-structure costs, as well as better efficiency and system scalability to meet capacity demand. Among the benefits of implementing a virtual-ized environment are lower operating costs as a result of improving hardware utilization. Because existing hardware is able to do more, fewer physical machines are required. Less hardware also reduces the amount of floor space required, and significantly lowers energy consumption.

To maximize system performance and IT investments, the require-ments of VMs must be aligned with the capabilities of the underlying hardware. By its design, server virtualization enables flexible system capacity to be increased quickly – without requiring additional capital investments and deployment time.

Since hardware management is greatly reduced with virtualization, additional server and desktop support personnel are not required, and IT departments shift from being strictly infrastructure providers to directors of business services.

Finally, most virtualization platforms offer features that help to increase service uptime. Virtualized environments can now takes steps to automatically recover the failed system and data if there is a problem. With fewer interruptions due to technical difficulties, business operations continue for clear productivity improvements.

INTRO TO APPLICATION VIRTUALIZATION

As was discussed earlier, mobility and the use of tablet PCs is transforming the way we use technology. As users adopt tablet PCs over desktop computers, enterprise users will need enterprise applications (e.g., financials, police records, permitting, GIS) on their tablet PCs. Currently, larger applications are either not available on the tablet PC, or they only offer limited functionality.

One shortcut to getting existing enterprise applications on tablet PCs is desktop and application virtualization. Like the server virtualization used in the data center, desktop virtualization moves an end-user desktop, complete with operating system and applications, into the data center.

Extending this approach to tablets PCs is fairly simple, especially if you already have a virtual desktop infrastructure in place. Rather than enhancing or replacing existing applications, install the appropriate client on your tablet device for access to your complete applications portfolio. Newer virtualization technologies allow for individual applications to be virtualized and presented to the user in a corporate "app store." On the backend, these applications run on a shared desktop image, limiting patching and maintenance to a small pool of images rather than requiring each user be provided with an individual desktop.

Application virtualization can provide a rapid way to get enterprise applications onto tablet PCs. However, since traditional desktop software assumes the use of full screens (e.g., 14-21-inches), which are significantly larger than the typical 5- to 10-inch tablet screen, and are keyboard- and mouse-centric instead of touch-centric, the use of application virtualization can be challenging for everyday use.

Up in the Cloud

If you are not thoroughly confused by now, there is another technology that takes advantage of virtualization to provide cost-effective application services to traditional desktop or tablet PC users – cloud computing.

There is no clear definition to cloud computing, yet the National Institute of Standards and Technology (NIST) has provided some definitions for the emerging set of technologies. According to NIST, the cloud model is characterized by:

Table 6-1 NIST Cloud computing definitions
<u>**NIST Cloud Computing Definitions**</u>

Broad network access	Accessible anywhere, by almost any device (e.g., smartphone, laptop, mobile devices, PDA).
Resource pooling	Cloud vendor computing resources (e.g., storage, processing, memory, network bandwidth, virtual machines) are pooled to serve multiple customers.
Rapid growth	Functionality can be rapidly provided and purchased in any quantity at any time.
Measured service	Ability to provide, monitor and control functionality based on a metric (e.g., storage, processing, bandwidth).

In this cloud service delivery model, the cloud vendor provides fully deployed applications. This service model eliminates the need for the local government to fund upfront capital costs of purchasing the hardware or pay software licensing fees. Cloud services can be deployed in varying degrees of accessibility and control.

Table 6-2 Types of cloud computing
Types of Cloud Computing

Private Cloud	This virtualized computing environment is for the exclusive use of a single organization. It might be owned, managed and operated by that organization, a third-party or a combination of the two. It might exist on or off the organization's premises.
Public Cloud	Open use for the general public, this virtualized environment might be owned, managed and operated by a business, academic or government organization or some combination of them, but it exists on the premises of the cloud provider.
Community Cloud	For exclusive use by a specific community of users from organizations that have shared concerns, such as mission, security requirements, policy and compliance considerations. It is owned, managed and operated by one or more of the organizations in the community, a third-party or some combination of them, and it might exist on or off the community's premises.
Hybrid Cloud	This virtualized environment includes two or more distinct cloud infrastructures (e.g., private, community, public) that remain unique entities, but are bound together by standardized or proprietary technology that enables the portability of data and applications.

While most local governments at first pursue cloud computing for financial benefits, the true benefit of cloud computing is the transformative effect that it has on the IT organization. With the reduced overhead associated with the maintenance of the infrastructure, IT can transition to becoming a more consultative organization that can truly empower the users for higher productivity. This approach reduces the amount of staff required to maintain the infrastructure, and increases available staff to provide business analysis services and deploy applications.

To Cloud…or Not

Having discussed both virtualization and cloud computing, *when does it make sense to transition to a virtualized or cloud environment, or stay with the onsite, dedicated server system?* Many management teams do not know how to assess the pros and cons of the data center hosting options, in order to make an informed decision. Here are some considerations when you are ready to start the discussion at your organization.

Table 6-3 The pros and cons of migrating to the Cloud
Into the Cloud

Pros	Cons
• Capital cost savings since most upfront hardware and software costs are assumed by the cloud provider.	• Less control of data security policies since data is under control of a third-party provider.
• Disaster recovery from hosting the applications at a remote site.	• Single point of failure through the network link.
• Reduced maintenance since most hardware administration can be performed through software functions.	• Potential performance limitations if the provider does not effectively tune their systems.
• Better scalability for IT growth.	• Recurring licensing costs.
• Simple migration of legacy applications.	• Steep learning curve for IT staff.

As noted earlier, the decision to support virtualization and cloud scenarios versus an onsite data center are determined by your IT staffing and available funding. Clearly, cloud services reduce upfront capital costs since you are not required to purchase the hardware infrastructure. There are also operational cost savings since daily hardware maintenance is handled by the cloud service provider. Although you will be losing direct control of your data and its systems, you will be geographically distributing your data, which means that you will have the ability to recover data if there is a disastrous physical or technical event onsite that destroys your file data.

There may be a steep learning curve for your IT staff to understand how to build and manage more complex virtualized environments, but once staff is up to speed, hardware resources can be optimized to reduce any inefficiency or waste. The organization will be able to quickly scale their compute capacity up or down, if needed, to improve performance or cut costs.

Virtual systems require ongoing investments in IT staff training. If senior management cannot fund the training or higher salaries to support the virtualization, a traditional server environmental may be more practical.

Table 6-4 Onsite data center pros and cons

<u>**Onsite Data Center**</u>

Pros	Cons
• Performance can be controlled and managed by internal staff on a single server eliminating performance limitations of too many applications on a single server.	• Capital expense. • Under-utilization of servers. • Limited ability to grow. • Hardware administration overhead.
• Separation of services since each application operates on its own server.	
• Security of data.	
• Less sophisticated technical skills required.	

Weighing the pros and cons of virtualization and cloud environments and onsite data centers is as unique as each organization and the people involved. For example, an organization with a simple application environment (e.g., finance, HR, payroll) with data that could be easily recovered and installed with a limited operations and maintenance budget, may find that they cannot afford the upfront costs and level of sophistication required to install and maintain a virtualized environment. They may be better off purchasing simple servers and having it maintained by a lower cost system administrator than paying for a sophisticated virtual server administrator who may be difficult to hire, costly to retain, and keep trained.

On the other hand, if the organization has a very complex application and server environment maintained by a large hardware and software staff, they may find that transitioning to virtualization, and eventually the cloud, may reduce costs and allow the IT staff to become more consultative and less of a hardware support organization.

The transformation of IT to a virtualized, cloud-based environment presents substantial initial cost to the government organization as your IT staff is trained and the technology needed for transition is acquired. The issues converting to the cloud are more organizational and strategic; the impact on staffing can be substantial and the shift should only be part of a larger strategic plan for IT that starts with a value-risk analysis (Chapter 14). Because of the many variables associated with this technology, a careful value-risk analysis should be performed.

Consider these questions as they relate to your government:

- *Will virtualization save us money?*
- *Do we have the IT resources to virtualize?*
- *Is senior management willing to invest in continuous IT staff training?*
- *Is the organization ready to outsource its data center in the Cloud?*
- *Are there any systems already in the Cloud?*
- *Do we have a disaster recovery strategy that addresses natural, intentional and unintentional threats?*

7

Integrated Municipal ERP and GIS

OVER THE LAST two decades, there has been a shift in how work is performed within local governments. Silo departments with separate functions and outputs have evolved into to a cooperative system of connected processes that cross functions and link organizational activities. Today, with increasingly tight budgets, business units are looking to improve their operational efficiency through the use of modern systems that help to manage financial and land management operations.

Integrated municipal enterprise resource planning (ERP) software systems can help local governments achieve these goals, but ERP decisions are complex involving business, financial, political, technical, process and organizational choices. Because these solutions are broad in their scope and reach deep within the organization, a broad-based governance group must be involved in the selection effort.

ERP SERVICE DELIVERY MODELS

Cloud computing offers a flexible approach to deploying an ERP system quickly and easily. Typically, ERP software can be delivered in three broad methods: on-premise, cloud and hybrid.

On-premise delivery models assume that businesses will license the ERP software and install it on computers at their location. ERP software users are responsible for buying computer hardware and software for these solutions. They are also responsible for applying any software upgrades, patches or fixes provided by the software vendor. IT staff provides system support, security, and database management.

Cloud delivery models allow the ERP software user to use application software on the vendor or a third-party's computing equipment. There are many different kinds of cloud delivery models though. Some simply provide a place for the software to run. Some clouds are operated by specialized ERP vendors. The most straightforward cloud solution is the hosted application. Otherwise, a thorough business analysis must be performed that weighs the value and risk of this approach versus others.

In this environment, an ERP software vendor makes its on-premises software available on a third-party cloud data center. Within this environment, customers do not have to acquire additional servers or other computing hardware. Depending on the provider, these cloud solutions may bundle database licenses or systems management software in their offering, which means the customer won't need to purchase them directly.

Is a cloud solution truly cheaper? The answer is yes – if the cloud provider also supplies the database software, security software, backup and other critical technologies. The most straightforward cloud solution is the hosted application.

The key benefits of this cloud delivery method are to eliminate large upfront computer hardware purchases for organizations, and reduce demands upon server management staff in IT. Pricing for ERP solutions is often done on a monthly basis and may be scaled up or down based on usage. Another benefit of this delivery model is that you retain control of upgrades, patches and fixes since the organization owns a copy of the ERP software. This approach affords more control and permits the user to make extensive modifications through configuration changes to the software.

Some cloud ERP services are multi-tenant, which means that only one copy of the application software is used by many customers concurrently, yet their data is kept separate. Since all maintenance work is performed by the cloud provider, there is no additional demand placed on existing IT staff and no additional IT personnel are required to support an ERP implementation.

Hybrid solutions represent the third kind of cloud delivery model for ERP. In a hybrid environment, software vendors may offer multiple methods for deploying the software. It can be used on-premises, hosted on the vendor's cloud, or on another firm's cloud. These solutions may also possess the flexibility to be initially implemented on a cloud and later moved back to a customer's own data center. This flexibility in going from on-demand to on-premises gives companies the ability to bring an application in-house to do more advanced business analytics.

Some hybrid ERP solutions can take a different form. For example, a vendor could offer certain modules (e.g., general ledger) as an on-premises application while other applications (e.g., citizen relationship management) are offered as hosted or on-demand solutions. These products are often designed to work together even though some ERP functionality and data may reside in the customer's data center; and, other data and functionality resides in a cloud environment.

Finally, some ERP vendors have started to deploy applications that are mobility-centric and take advantage of the tablet PCs touch capabilities. When ERP vendors begin to convert their legacy systems to cloud-based mobility, the true use of tablet computing will be achieved in the enterprise.

GIS Transforms

Within government, the need to manage land based assets is fundamental. In order to provide support for land based asset management, governments have been deploying geographic information systems (GIS) over the past 20 years. GIS provides the capability to gather different types of information based on proximity and analyze their relationships. By integrating hardware, software and data, GIS can capture, manage, analyze and display all forms of geographical information. Data can be viewed, interpreted and visualized in many ways. It can help us identify relationships, patterns and trends in the form of maps, reports and charts.

For example, in researching ground water quality issues, information can be collected on soil type, depth to ground water, fertilizer usage, cropping patterns, and irrigation usage to model the impact of irrigated, fertilized crops on ground water quality in a given area.

In short, GIS helps organizations to analyze data visually with graphics, which can make complex issues easier to understand and to predict potential outcomes. Additionally, GIS can simplify communications with local government councils and other local government personnel by presenting complex data in a visual format that is easily shared and quickly understood.

One of the most promising and cost-effective applications of GIS technology is the modernization of local government land records maintenance and access. In addition to land record modernization, there are numerous other potential local government applications of GIS technology (e.g., emergency response, public health and safety, zoning, taxation, street and utility maintenance). The property parcel and land record information maintained by local governments is another GIS database needed by a wide variety of state, local and federal agencies, and private entities.

The active link that GIS provides between databases and maps greatly facilitates the maintenance of mapped information on dynamic features such as property parcels. With GIS, a County Assessor can easily update a property parcel map with new information on an easement for a buried cable and tie it back to a database with the owner's information.

In order to maximize the use of this technology, IT has to work with users to bridge the gap between the complexity of the GIS application and the user's needs to get the job done. This requires IT to have both architecture planning and systems analysis skills that are not readily present in most traditional infrastructure-focused IT organizations.

KEEPING IT SAFE

As technology becomes more integrated into the way local government operates, the systems managed by IT become more critical. Keeping the systems safe from threats has become one of the key functions that IT must perform.

Although threats to information systems are evolving and abundant, they can all be broken down into three categories.

Table 7-1 Threat categories to information systems
Threat Categories to Information Systems

Natural threats	"Acts of God" that include lightning, floods, earthquakes, tornadoes, extreme temperatures, hurricanes, storms, etc.
Intentional threats	Computer crimes when property or information is damaged on purpose including espionage, identity theft, credit card crime, and denial of service attacks.
Unintentional threats	Unauthorized or accidental modification of software including accidentally deleting key files or a power supply failure.

IT must plan for each of these types of threats with systems and procedures that address and recover from the breech or failure. With evolving mobile technologies, the threats are becoming ever more complex and difficult to contain.

Consider these questions as they relate to your government:

- *Is the integrated municipal ERP (e.g., finance and land management) meeting our operational needs?*
- *Is our GIS isolated in a department or is it enterprise-ready?*
- *How safe and secure are our systems?*
- *Are backup systems and recovery procedures in place?*
- *Have recovery capabilities of mission critical systems been assessed?*
- *Are fallback manual processes in place in case of a catastrophic system failure?*

8

The Promise of Performance Improvement

*W*HY DO WE *have all this technology anyway? Has it really helped improve our performance in a measurable and meaningful way? Have we helped our citizens improve their quality of life, or the quality of their interactions with us?*

Over the last few decades, we have collected a lot of data. Generating reports with complex systems has required support from technical personnel who do not necessarily understand the business problem. Information gathered took a while to analyze and answer important business questions. By then, they were not very helpful or actionable.

Managers receive the collected data in customized and costly reports. The reporting tools are not intuitive and require training to use. These systems only regurgitate data, sometimes summarized, but never information that is actionable. Worst of all, by the time the managers get the data, it's six to eight weeks old so the window to take real action based on the data has passed.

To respond to senior management's requests for performance metrics, managers have spent hours upon hours reviewing data, and comparing it to known baselines and benchmarks. They have established Key Performance Indicators (KPI) and Balanced Scorecard Measures. But managers have a job to do and cannot afford to spend valuable time analyzing old data that produces little-to-no real outcome for the business. For example, managers can tell you that they were at 80% of planned budget…two months ago. This approach is far too reactive to be truly effective.

There is hope. The next generation of systems to be released, both self-hosted and cloud-based, are moving past the delayed data reporting model. They offer state-of-the-art interfaces that often include dashboards. Think of your organization as a car; you have multiple tools you can use to affect performance when driving, and the dashboard provides real-time information about how it's running. With these new systems, your dashboard gives you a view of your organization's performance today based the information you want to track (e.g., finances, budgets, permits, licenses, work order completions, complaints).

Equipped with this viewpoint, performance management can start with accurate information and clear thinking. Performance metrics established for each department; can be baselined and even benchmarked. Most importantly, measures can be taken on a regular basis to ensure that the methods employed by management are resulting in continuous improvement.

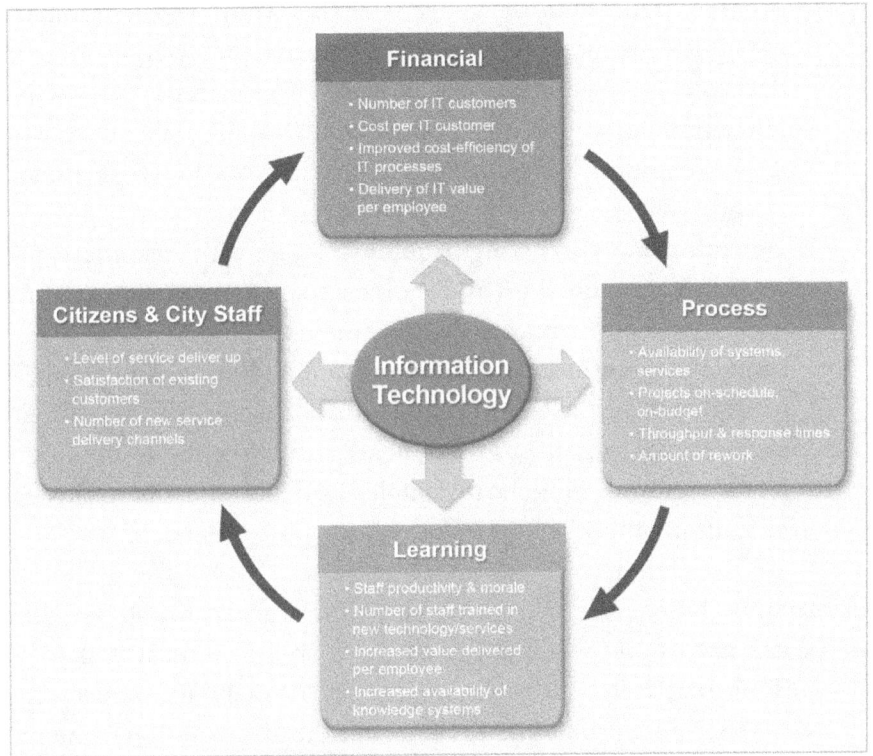

Figure 8-1 Balanced Scorecard for departments

Strategic planning for IT clearly is a common theme throughout this book. The IT Strategic Plan identifies the vision and the mission of the IT department, as well as the services it provides to achieve that mission. It also defines, for a limited planning horizon such as five years, what the IT department will do to move the vision of the organization forward – specifically its goals, projects and standards.

How can the IT department use performance management?

- **Showing progress.** With goals and standards set in the IT Strategic Plan, IT Management needs to track and report on progress against those goals. Whether your organization utilizes a governance group to make priority, policy and standards decisions regarding IT, or whether IT simply reports to Senior Management, reporting against goals enables IT to provide its stakeholders with an understanding of the department's progress.

- **Detecting and correcting problems.** Issues with customers, processes and technologies all become apparent when you are tracking specific performance measurements.
- **Improving continuously.** Tracking and analyzing data allows IT to understand the effectiveness and efficiency of the strategy, architecture, organization, policies, processes and technologies it has deployed. This clarity enables IT make adjustments instead of waiting on budget cycles or catastrophic events.

Performance management is fun when things are running smoothly and we can report on successes; but when an organization is challenged and working reactively, it is time-consuming to track and report – and who wants to report problems? Keep in mind, this is the time when it's needed most. There's a business philosophy from the quality management movement: *If you're not measuring it, you can't improve it.* We need to monitor performance measures closely, especially when there are issues, to ensure we are addressing the root of the problem.

What do we need to know when we're establishing our performance measures? At a minimum, we want to know:

- *Who is accountable for tracking and reporting on the performance? To whom are they accountable?*
- *What analysis are they performing on the data? What information is being reported from that analysis? Are we using baselines or benchmarks in our analysis?*
- *How will the information be reported? How frequently?*

What sort of performance measures should the IT department be tracking? There are dozens of potential measures to be used that should be spelled out in the IT Strategic Plan. We should focus our performance measures on those services specified in the IT Strategic Plan to understand:

- *Are the services meeting the needs of our customers?*
- *Are our customers using the services?*
- *Are the services producing the results we intended?*

You should start with a few performance measures that you can easily track, and build upon these over time. In the end, the organization should be tracking the IT Department's performance in the areas detailed in Table 8-1.

Table 8-1 Performance measures for IT

<u>Area</u>	<u>Performance Standard Example</u>
Management	Governance Committee meets at least once a quarter to review and adjust current IT priorities.
Standards	A PC replacement program has been established to ensure that all equipment is compliant with IT's standards, and that hardware is replaced on a timely basis.
Policies & Processes	Core policies and processes have been developed and are tested when used. Deviations from optimum performance are reported to the Change Advisory Board for continuous improvement.
Security	Security standards have been developed, which include diagnostic tools, monitoring tools, intrusion detection systems, firewalls,

encryption, secure email, and anti-virus protection. Deviations for optimum performance of these standards are reported to IT Security for analysis and potential correction.

Applications

Formal process for new applications acquisition has been approved by the IT Governance Committee, requiring the development of specifications prior to vendor solicitation and evaluation. Deviations are reported to the IT Governance Committee.

Network & Telephony

Processes have been established to ensure the integrity of the network to minimize downtime. Deviations greater than 0.01% of time per month must be reported to the IT Governance Committee.

Recoverability

Disaster recovery standards and processes have been developed and are tested on a quarterly basis. Deviations from optimum are reported to the Change Advisory Board for continuous improvement.

Customer Service

Customer satisfaction with the IT Department is measured through annual surveys (solicited) and through help desk anonymous satisfaction feedback (unsolicited). The results are reported to the IT Governance Committee when they meet each quarter.

Consider these questions as they relate to your government:

- *Does IT have performance standards in place? Do they relate to its strategic plan?*
- *What tools does IT have to measure performance? Are they labor intensive or automated?*
- *Are the customers' needs being met? How do you know?*
- *How does IT know where to focus its energies for performance improvement?*

9

Architect for Sustainability

G ONE ARE THE days when local government ran their entire IT function on a single mainframe. One platform IT organizations could be managed with minimal staff, yet provided equally minimal functional value to the users since most of the work was done on paper and the system was used for reporting purposes only.

Today's IT environments are incredibly complex. We've moved into cloud computing, Web services, databases, multiple applications, authentication domains and mobility. We have not, however, removed many of the legacy systems in the IT environment. Instead, we've added more and more, making IT even more complex and confusing. Management is now realizing that we are reaching a critical point where complexity is increasing costs, as well as degrading the quality of service.

The way to achieve a lower overall total cost of ownership (TCO) is to carefully consider how all of the technologies that support the business solution interact. Imagine listening to an orchestra where the musicians are all playing in different keys. Music happens when a standard key is defined, and the musicians are all playing from the same music score. This "orchestration" of components defines the IT architecture. IT architecture models, although having the same goals, can be daunting to implement.

For example, Microsoft® introduced a reference architecture guide to assist IT planners in developing Windows Server® architecture. Similar to other guidelines, such as the FEAF (Federal Enterprise Architecture Framework) and TOGAF (The Open Group Architecture Framework), this reference architecture guide is a complex set of recommendations, spanning more than 3,500 pages of content. This material, while valuable, is difficult to read and understand, and even more challenging to implement. IT architectural design continues to evolve, becoming more practical and easier to apply to real-world situations.

In our example, the Microsoft guide provides procedures for all IT and end-user services (e.g., security, networking, management) as shown in Table 9-1.

Table 9-1 End user services descriptions and examples

Architecture	**Description**	**Technology Examples**
Network	Design considerations for deploying a network infrastructure to support communication within the enterprise	Routers, switches, servers, DNS (domain name system), DHCP (dynamic host configuration protocol), replication
Security	Security strategy for security zoning, policies, procedures	Perimeter and internal firewalls, Web proxy services, caching, Microsoft Active Directory
Management	Enhancement of technology architecture to support applications	Microsoft Active Directory, remote management tools

Storage	Based on Microsoft Operations Framework (MOF), the guiding principles for the management and operations of the infrastructure	DAS (direct-attached storage), NAS (network attached storage), SAN (storage area network), Cloud Storage
Application Infrastructure	Architectural choices for consolidating and/or centralizing storage	Web services, Microsoft SQL Server, .NET

The IT architecture development process should consider the current standards on which the existing organizational systems operate. To minimize complexity in the data center, the IT architecture should consolidate as much of the IT architecture from the same vendor as possible. The efficiency of technology and architecture can be improved by reducing the number of vendors required to maintain your IT architecture. Managing a larger number of vendors requires more time on the part of IT managers to coordinate activities and is tremendously inefficient. Identify a few key vendors, ensure they understand your goals and requirements, and delegate parts of the project to them.

Simple IT architectures can deliver effective technologies that are easier to deploy and maintain. In particular, focus on proven technologies that are widely available and priced less. When technologies are widely available, a greater number of people are familiar with the technology, so there is no need to resort to expensive consultants who know specialized technologies.

Management should be innovative about business, not technology. It's easy to fall victim to hype, but sometimes investing in the latest technologies and gadgets brings the biggest price tag with expensive people to support it. Worse, it can add unnecessary complexity and cost to maintaining to your IT architecture. Since governments have low risk tolerance, it's best to be on the cutting-edge without bleeding. IT architectural designers must keep both value and risk in mind.

Maintain Your Standards

Basing your IT architecture on prominent standardized systems is a practical strategic decision. Standardizing platforms and applications drives down costs and improves the simplicity of managing the architecture. There should be integrated platforms and standards in the network, applications, databases, development languages, and end-user devices. The internal IT team can easily become knowledgeable of standardized systems – if they aren't already – without requiring ongoing specialized training or external vendor support.

Technology can streamline business processes through application integration. Focus on infrastructure management technologies that support and integrate with key processes, making those processes more efficient. Not only does it save staff time, but fewer applications will support more functions. The best investments concentrate on processes that reach widely across the organization.

The IT architecture should be based on a grouping of technologies that are easily supported by economically stable vendors. Established vendors with the largest market share who have been in the industry for a long time are ideal because the systems are widely available with a strong support ecosystem.

Preventing IT problems is far less costly and time-consuming than fixing IT problems, so invest early in testing and managing how the systems are released to the users. There should be a special focus on eliminating unplanned work. Responding to IT emergencies is the most inefficient and expensive work that an IT department does. It is time-consuming to troubleshoot problems, and then to repair the problems. It has become all too common to expect downtime, but technologies today are able to handle high volumes of changes without outages or IT emergencies.

New technologies should be self-monitoring and grow with your organization. Once you launch a new program, you don't want to waste the time and resources you saved in maintenance on tracking the effectiveness of the new program. New technologies should be able to adapt easily to changing processes or measurements in your environment, and automatically capture key metrics.

Consider these questions as they relate to your government:

- *What is our process for developing the architecture?*
- *Under what standard architecture do most of the available mission critical applications operate?*
- *Do we research the industry for trends and direction?*
- *Are there established standards and minimal number of vendors at every level of our architecture (e.g., servers, network, desktops, operating systems, databases)?*
- *Do we stick to buying to our standards or do we buy the lowest price items?*

10

Manage Through IT Governance

A S THE TECHNOLOGY environment has become more complex the risks have increased. Yet users are demanding greater value from the limited, and many times, diminishing IT resources. IT must maximize value and optimize benefits affordably with an acceptable level of risk. As shown in Figure 10.1, IT Governance is the management methodology by which IT can control the variables necessary to achieve the goals of senior management and maintain its strategic alignment with its customers.

Figure 10-1 Role of IT governance

As an ongoing process for setting priorities, IT Governance is concerned with two outcomes: 1) delivering value to the business; and 2) avoiding risk. Strategic alignment of IT to the business, adequate resources, and monitoring progress all help to achieve these outcomes.

IT managers use their management skills and experience to work together with users to optimize value and reduce risks for any project within the portfolio. The Governance Committee helps to streamline the technology prioritization process for senior management by requiring each project to have a sponsor, who must explain the value of the project for the organization; and evaluating all technology projects collectively so that relative value-risk can be compared at the same time.

Most IT projects fail when the requirements are not carefully considered before a project is started. Instituting a formal process with a project sponsor and IT Governance review ensures that when IT receives a project request, the scope of work has been sufficiently clarified. (We will discuss more about project selection and prioritization in Chapter 15.) With a Governance Plan developed by the committee, departments must also thoroughly think through their IT requests before submitting requisitions.

Allocating Resources

Once a project is approved by the Governance Committee, the project budget may be allocated between the user department and IT. As budgets become distributed, the management of technology investments becomes more complex.

Typically, IT represents 4% to 8% of the local government or county budgets – a significant investment. In order to show value to the organization, IT must be able to effectively track and manage enterprise-wide technology spending and its direct business value.

Since business management is starting to drive more of the technology deployments, their involvement in setting technology priorities has become more important. Nevertheless, IT is still responsible for managing the technology infrastructure. A thoughtful and collaborative approach to technology management is needed. When individual departments make the technology decisions, they usually lack a detailed understanding of the technology, as well as the priorities beyond their own department. When IT makes technology decisions, they may lack a full appreciation of their business impact. This shared decision process focuses on value delivery, and is one of the drivers toward better IT governance.

While IT governance has emerged as a tool to engage the entire organization in making IT investment decisions, IT must lead the charge. It is IT's responsibility to align with its customers and to show value to the organization for the investments.

DOING MORE WITH LESS

Problem

After the housing bubble burst in 2009, the Town of Jupiter, Florida was experiencing budgetary pressures like other local governments. In response, the Town needed to lower its overall operating budget to maintain the positive fiscal health it had always enjoyed.

At the same time, the Chief of Police, who managed the lion's share of the Town's budget, was looking for ways to improve operational integration and data sharing with other agencies in the surrounding jurisdictions. Given the resource challenges faced by officials, the Town decided to explore consolidating their communications center and records management system with the nearby Town of Palm Beach Gardens.

Plan of Action

The most important ingredient required to successfully integrate a system across the jurisdictions was establishing a governance process. Firm governance ensures that technical solutions align with strategic objectives. The inter-local agreement between the Town Councils addressed the rules of engagement for working together, while the details were negotiated directly between the jurisdictions.

Working with the senior Town staffs assigned to the project, a service level agreement was created that specified service delivery terms between the jurisdictions, agreed performance metrics, and the escalation steps if performance was unacceptable.

Consultants at Sciens worked closely with the jurisdictions to draft a technical architecture, at both the network and applications level, to identify how the system would support all teams - everyone from dispatcher to mobile officer to records clerk. Recognizing that the software vendor's project plan was limited to software installation and that the Town's success was dependent upon many other factors, the Town engaged consultants to manage the overall consolidation. This began with validation of the design and identifying the requirements for the consolidation.

With the new system in place, the consultants handled project management of the consolidation between the towns. Every aspect of the project was defined in a detailed project plan which included specific task assignments and contingencies outside the control of the project team (e.g., FCC licenses). Weekly meetings were conducted to review progress. The team quickly came together holding each other accountable for the fast and successful deployment of the computer-aided dispatch (CAD), records management systems (RMS), and integrated networks.

Results

Now, the Town of Jupiter is being dispatched from Palm Beach Gardens, and the two towns are supported by separate instances of the RMS. Through this process, the Town of Jupiter saved over a quarter of a million dollars in project implementation costs alone. The consolidation saved the Town of Jupiter over $1.5 million by avoiding the purchase of a new CAD/RMS, and related hardware and support. Projects including the move to a new data center, WAN, and modernization of GIS were completed by the existing staff with no staff turnover.

Consider these questions as they relate to your government:

- *Are all IT expenditures centrally tracked?*
- *Do the departments engage IT in planning and budgeting for their technology projects?*
- *Does IT engage the departments in developing the collaborative management structure that defines the responsibilities of IT and the departments?*
- *Does IT periodically update the strategic vision for technology in order to assist departments with understanding evolving trends and the effect on operations?*

11

Organize for Success

EFFECTIVE ORGANIZATIONAL STRUCTURE is the cornerstone of a healthy enterprise. The best organizational structures leverage the Governance principle of the Clear Thinking Model for setting business priorities. The senior management team is engaged in clarifying priorities, off-loading low level tasks, and allocating resources for IT to execute. With clarity, the entire organization works collaboratively for a common goal.

Strong leadership is also fundamental toward building an effective IT department. It sets the goals and expectations for the team, and fosters a sense of ownership for their work. Regular communication and incentives – like bonuses, comp time, training and recognition – motivate employees and help to deliver a higher quality work product.

A change in cultural mindset is typically required for significant performance improvements. Most people need to understand why change must happen before they can embrace a new strategy and approach. As the role of IT management becomes more strategic, they will be equipped to communicate the opportunities available through the right technologies. Once they can move beyond being just the "computer guy," you have taken the first step toward advancing IT.

ORGANIZATION & CLARITY

An operation is only as efficient as its processes, and as effective as the organization implementing them. With IT Governance in place, reactive IT cases can be minimized.

Model the organization around standard processes, not around people or personalities. Designing an organization around individuals creates weaknesses in the structure. People can quit, retire, go on vacation, become ill or even win the lottery. You don't want your organization to grind to a stop because a key individual is not available. Focus on building a solid organization with efficient processes to strengthen the operations.

Although somewhat intimidating, senior management must take responsibility for IT by monitoring it like any other professional business function. Managing an IT department involves the following:

1. Evaluate the IT department's activities to confirm that they are supporting organizational goals.
2. Define what services the organization needs the IT department to provide (e.g., LAN, desktop support).
3. Define what services the organization does not need the IT department to provide that can be outsourced (e.g., project management, network monitoring).
4. Assess the IT staff to ensure that they have the appropriate skills and experience to perform their jobs.
5. Establish S.M.A.R.T. goals for the IT department using metrics associated with the services defined in Step 2.
6. Hold the IT department accountable for achieving its goals.

S.M.A.R.T. Goals

Specific

Measurable

Attainable

Relevant

Time-Specific

Once IT is supporting overall organizational goals, the role of IT must be explained clearly to the entire organization. In a few government organizations where IT is run as a business, everyone is clear about the services IT provides, how to ask for help, and who their contact person is. There are regularly scheduled meetings to gauge their satisfaction of IT services, understand their business goals, and most importantly what IT can do to help them achieve their goals.

ESTABLISHING A CULTURE OF QUALITY IN IT

A knowledgeable and efficient Help Desk will relieve a lot of pressure from the IT organization from reactive, firefighting support. Help Desks can handle a lot of the initial support requirements without forwarding them to higher level IT staff, which ensures that IT remains focused on delivering the tools and architecture that improve the productivity of the organization.

Data obtained from the *Day in the Life* analysis, and corroborated through end user interviews, indicate that nearly 53% of the overall IT organization's time is dedicated to reactive problem resolution and performing reactive Service Desk work.

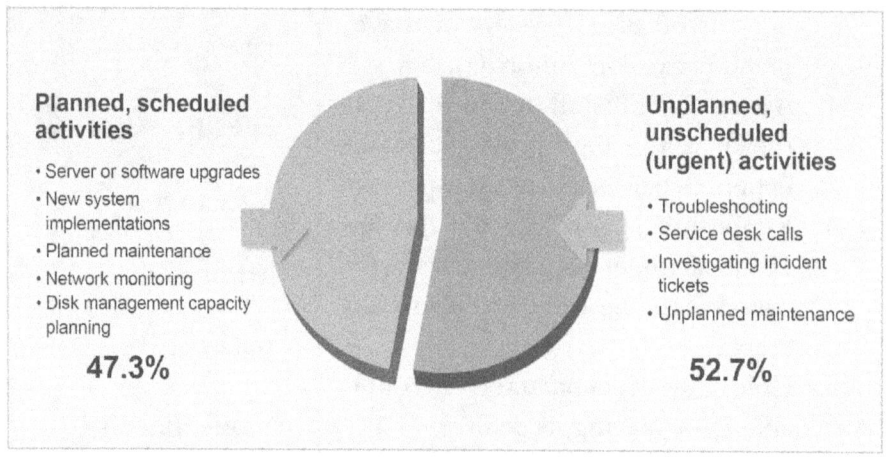

Figure 11-1 Planned versus unplanned IT activities

By contrast, research indicates that high performing IT organizations establish priorities through a centralized clearinghouse and deal with minimal unplanned and distruptive emergencies[9]:

A Culture of Change Management
In high performing IT organizations, staff implements changes by going to a change management board and requesting the change. Surprisingly, this process was not viewed as bureaucratic or needlessly slowing projects down or decreasing the quality of work. Instead, it was viewed as absolutely critical to the organization maintaining its high performance since it weeded out changes that were not important from those that were, and ensured that changes were effectively communicated to all affected.

Minimal Unplanned Work
High performing IT organizations provide more consistent and predictable service levels, and they consistently spend less than 5% of their time on unplanned and urgent work. In contrast, the Information Technology Process Institute benchmarking shows that typical IT organizations spend between 35-45% of their time on unplanned and unscheduled work.

Investigations into the relationship between organizational effectiveness and quality were performed by Kim S. Cameron from the Department of Management at Brigham Young University. Cameron and his colleagues studied the quality culture/organizational effectiveness balance among automotive, electronics, and educational industries[10].

---

9 The Visible Ops Handbook Implementing ISIL in 4 Practical and Auditable Steps, Information Technology Process Institute, Kevin Behr, Gene Kim and George Spafford.

10 Enhancing Organizational Performance (1997), Commission on Behavioral and Social Sciences and Education, Daniel Druckman, Jerome E. Singer, and Harold Van Cott, Editors, Committee on Techniques for the Enhancement of Human Performance Commission on Behavioral and Social Sciences and Education National Research Council, NATIONAL ACADEMY PRESS, 2101 Constitution Avenue, N.W., Washington, D.C. 20418.

Quality culture promotes a set of values, principles, and definitions related to achieving high quality. It represents a way of working, a way of thinking, a personal commitment, and a lifestyle that is shared by members throughout the organization. Cameron determined that organizations with an advanced quality culture (e.g., error prevention, perpetual creative quality) had higher levels of organizational effectiveness than organizations with a less advanced quality culture.

Table 11-1 A model of quality cultures in three stages

Stage	Service Delivery	Customers
Error Detection	1. Avoid mistakes 2. Reduce waste, rework, repair 3. Detect problems 4. Focus on outputs	1. Do not annoy customers 2. Respond to complaints efficiently and accurately 3. Assess customer satisfaction after engagement 4. Focus on needs and requirements
Error Prevention	1. Expect zero defects 2. Prevent errors and mistakes 3. Hold everyone accountable 4. Focus on processes and root causes	1. Satisfy customers and exceed expectations 2. Eliminate problems in advance 3. Involve customers in design 4. Focus on preferences or nice-to-have attributes
Perpetual Creative Quality	1. Constant improvement and escalating standards 2. Concentrate on things gone right 3. Emphasize breakthroughs 4. Focus on improvement in suppliers, customers, processes	1. Expect lifelong loyalty 2. Surprise and delight customers 3. Anticipate expectations 4. Create new preferences

IT organizations with a high volume of unplanned work or a large number of fixes being done through the Help Desk indicates that their focus is on trying to meet the deployment goals without monitoring the quality. Users end up calling back numerous times for support through the Help Desk, or calling the original project managers directly. Either way, the customer is seeking remedial support in an environment that treats the symptoms, not the disease. Once a project is completed, the IT staff should move on to other projects and no longer worry about the resolved project.

MANAGEMENT LEADERSHIP

Historically, IT has played an important role for local government in providing a secure technical infrastructure, while minimizing costs. On the other hand, while IT has been focused on controlling the technical environment and its related costs, the technology needs of local government departments have evolved.

The local government departments' external customers (e.g., residents, businesses, visitors) have become more technically sophisticated. Their transactional expectations have changed from in-person to online. They expect instant access to information and forms in a user-friendly, transactional interface like Amazon.com. In addition, interactions between local government personnel and residents require a high degree of flexibility and bandwidth for training, file transfer, and media tracking.

> *Innovation has nothing to do with how many R&D dollars you have, it's not about money, it's about the people you have, how you're led.*
> *Steve Jobs*

Many local government IT departments have not supported this evolution, and customers and departments do not feel properly supported. The infrastructure IT provides today is a highly complex technical environment that can potentially hamper day-to-day local government operations.

Management, culture, operations, (i.e., infrastructure, process) and staffing, (i.e., organization, skills and knowledge) within government tend to be resistant to technological innovation and change, and unable to lead the city's technological transformation. The IT staff must be committed to leading the transformation; while management should provide the leadership and governance practices that will ensure success.

IT organizations have been generally focused on technology and control, but they need to focus on management and leadership – the focus of Transforming Government. Moving forward, many senior managers have made it clear that IT must balance customer needs and departments with cost containment and security. Translate the strategy into action, in terms of what is done, how it is done, and what is accomplished. Simplify highly complex technical environment to minimize support requirements, and build bridges to the departments through extensive use of customer-focused business analysts.

Successful IT organizations exhibiting management leadership are able to understand and balance the needs of both business process and technology. IT leaders spend more time with user departments to understand their needs and explore possible technology solutions, which earns the respect of their colleagues and fosters an attitude of innovation.

Effective IT leaders know how to simplify and communicate complex ideas clearly. Advanced technologies and business processes can be daunting to typical users. By simplifying their environment on standardized hardware, integrated software, and streamlined processes, the environment is easier to manage and use.

Technology is inherently flawed and designed to eventually fail. Building strong relationships throughout the organization provides understanding and goodwill that helps IT maintain their reputation when systems fail. Strong relationships are built on trust – two-way trust.

IT should invest the time to work with people at every level of the organization and build mutual trust.

Culture of Success

Collaboration between government functions helps to integrate processes, including IT operations and IT security, and enables a smoother working relationship between IT and the business users. Clearly, collaboration and communication ensure that IT efforts are focused on common objectives and deliver the functionality the organization needs.

Too often we direct our attention inward at points of frustration, however to remain effective, IT should concentrate on customer or business needs. Large leaps in organizational effectiveness come from big picture thinking to create new, improved realities. Opportunities for creative discussions to brainstorm new ideas give rise to a more productive and efficient local government.

TRANSFORMATIONAL PLANS THROUGH VISIONARY LEADERSHIP

Problem

A fast growing city was experiencing problems with its technology systems. Network outages were increasing, and applications just didn't meet business needs. By their own admission, local government management didn't understand what the IT department did. They simply wanted everything to work, and wanted to adopt technologies to simplify their processes. They wanted to become a technology leader, respected for their practical, cost-conscious leadership in applying technologies to improve services. IT management was repeatedly asked for an improvement plan. Management believed that such a plan would provide department managers with confidence that their issues would be addressed; it would assure city management that the technology investments they had been making for a decade were being maintained. Not receiving a plan from IT, city management looked outside the organization for help.

Plan of Action

Often, the assumption is the people are the problem, but many times it is more complicated. To determine the true source of the problem, an assessment of the environment, the technology, and more importantly, the people and processes were required. The findings reviewed with IT management indicated that although the technology infrastructure had weaknesses, it was the IT organization, its culture and its processes that were at the heart of the problem. Specifically, the culture was defensive, reactive and entrenched.

In conjunction with city management, substantial time was spent educating the IT department in what the city wanted to achieve and how they could lead that effort. With IT management, we were looking for the "Ah-ha!" moment, when their passion ignites and enables them to lead their team to change. When this realization is missing, it's usually because the IT team does not see a problem, or does not want to change. We have had much success over the years inspiring that "Ah-ha!" moment.

At that point, city management took responsibility for the employee, and with assistance, the selection process for new

IT management began. Together with the departments and the IT staff, an IT Strategic Plan was developed.

Results

The new IT director was able become acquainted with the technology needs of the management team, the technical environment, and the staff. With that knowledge, the IT director was able to use the IT plan as a foundation, and provide the needed leadership to further improve the plan. Local government business is dependent upon technology. A successful IT department is dependent upon experienced, knowledgeable leadership that can execute a plan.

Consider these questions as they relate to your government:

- *Does IT staff often look like they are responding to an emergency?*
- *Does IT have measurable goals that tie back to the broader organizational goals?*
- *Do IT projects seem to take longer than they should?*
- *Does IT management have a clear strategic vision that is communicated to staff and senior management?*

12

To Outsource or to Insource?
That is the Question.

T HE INTRODUCTION OF digital government has brought positive results to the community and internal operations, however with increased expectations for services, many of the changes required additional work from the end-user staff. For organizations unaccustomed or resistant to change, this process can result in significant turnover and/or failed projects if not managed effectively. The impact of the digital government wave on local government can result in:

- Increasing demands on staff
- Reengineering processes
- Changing staff roles
- Improving process efficiency[11]

---

11 Smith, Russell L. "The Electronic Village: Local Governments and E-Governments at the Dawn of a New Millennium." Washington, D.C.: International City/County Management Association, 2001.

The lessons of digital government show that resourcing must be reconsidered. In the older model, the rule of thumb was that insourcing was usually cheaper than outsourcing. This is not always true today.

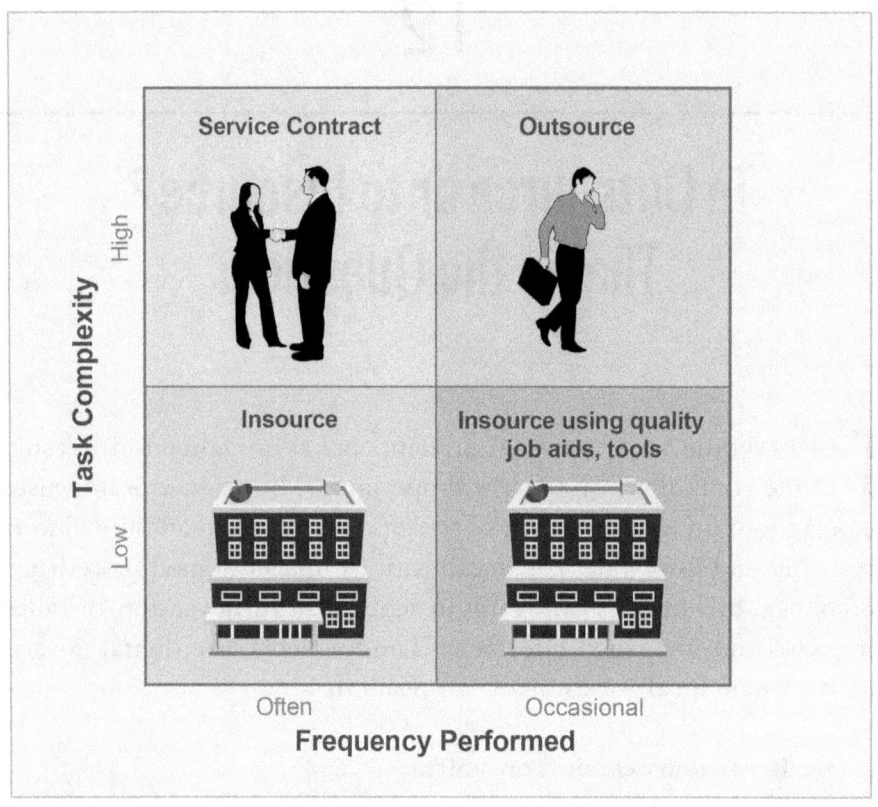

Figure 12-1 Complexity of task versus frequency performed comparison

Increasing specialization and complexity of systems many times means that outsourcing costs less. Tasks that are performed infrequently and have a high degree of specialization are best outsourced; however management and quality control should always remain insourced.

The examples in Figure 12-1 illustrate the task complexity and frequency balance between insourcing and outsourcing:

- High Complexity, Performed Occasionally: Website re-development, call management analysis
- High Complexity, Performed Often: Website maintenance and servicing
- Low Complexity, Performed Occasionally: Adding an extension to the phone system
- Low Complexity, Performed Often: System administration on the servers

IT is concerned about controlling information confidentiality. The problem is that controlling information is often confused with controlling information systems. Just because servers and computers are safely within the physical walls of government buildings does not guarantee that the information is safe. We hear news reports about sensitive information being compromised when notebook computers are lost by employees, and we also hear about hackers illegally accessing sensitive information even though they've never set foot in the building.

To be clear, outsourcing technical services does not threaten the control of information. As discussed, governments can take advantage of expanded external cloud services to outsource their application environments. In many cases, the external services have taken additional steps to ensure security and are far more secure than even internally located hardware. Outsourcing certain applications or services also relieves some of the burden of work from internal IT teams, and is usually less expensive in the long-term than adding more IT staff.

The best approach is to select the target areas for outsourcing and build relationships with providers who consistently deliver the same level of service – or better – than you can deliver. Incorporate external partners into all aspects of your operating processes, but be careful to not make the mistake of allowing them to operate independently. Contract for specific levels of service, with measurable outputs, and manage against those service levels. Always maintain constant communication regarding evolving procedures and performance against your success metrics and business goals.

Outsourcing Considerations

Determining the best path forward with technology can be difficult. Infrastructure is becoming more complex. In some cases, it makes sense to hire an experienced, independent third-party that is well-versed in industry best practices to evaluate your strategic plan, processes and technologies. Working with numerous organizations facing similar challenges enables them to quickly diagnose problems and identify practical solutions that work.

Nevertheless, any vendor you hire should have the specific knowledge and experience needed for your situation. They should provide examples of similar projects they have completed, as well as references. If they did a good job, there shouldn't be a problem discussing their performance with customers. Don't forget to ask their customers about the relationship they had with the vendor. How a vendor behaves toward customers can be just as important as what they do.

Cloud Computing Outsourcing

Many of the risks associated with cloud computing are similar to those found in local government computing today. Managing the risks of outsourcing key computing capabilities must be well planned. To minimize risk, it's important to have a clear understanding with the way the cloud provider runs its organization, as well as the architecture in place, security measures and policies. Examples of cloud computing risks that local government IT manager should consider are listed in Table 12-1.

Table 12-1 Potential cloud computing risks

<u>Potential Cloud Computing Risks</u>

- Vendor history and experience
- Contract lock-in
- Data ownership and custodian responsibilities
- Disaster recovery and business continuity
- Assurance over cloud services
- Information security and privacy
- Legal and contractual issues
- Longevity of suppliers
- Capability of suppliers
- Stability of technology
- Common performance standards
- Performance monitoring
- Regulatory compliance

MITIGATE RISKS THROUGH OUTSOURCING CONTRACTS

In any outsourcing relationship, whether directly with an individual vendor or a complete cloud deployment, it is critical to have clearly defined terms and processes. When working with vendors, the Statement of Work (SOW) defines your rights as a customer and your relationship with the vendor. The SOW should list specific deliverables and timelines for completion of the work.

A clear SOW is important for two primary reasons: first, it ensures that both the vendor and the government representative are clear on expectations *before* the work starts; and second, there is no uncertainty about when the vendor is failing to perform the terms of the contract *after* the work has started.

In the case of outsourcing operations or applications to a vendor, such as a cloud provider, the Service Level Agreement (SLA) is the primary document that defines service levels with measurable outputs.

Depending on the type of outsourcing relationship, these outputs can include the number of transactions processed, timeliness of processes, age of issues remaining unresolved. The SLA provides specific goals defining success.

The entire outsourcing contract (e.g., SOW, SLA, terms and conditions) is a legal document that establishes the scope, terms, conditions, legal liabilities, responsibilities and remedies between the parties. A well-defined contract that clearly describes the key issues is essential to a successful outsourcing relationship. In the case of outsourced cloud-based systems, areas defined should include:

- Ownership or lease of hardware, software licenses, etc.
- Ownership of data and access to data upon contract termination
- Recourse in the event of data breach
- Ownership of intellectual property (IP), such as applications developed by the contractor for the local government, or those applications developed by the local government to run in the cloud vendor's data center
- Hiring of vendor staff by the local government, or vice versa
- Rights to audit the environment and third-party assurance of controls
- Billing
- Recourse for, and remediation of, unsatisfactory performance
- Renewal or termination of services

In the end, any outsourcing vendor should be aligned with your goals, and deliver services that provide business value. You should expect the vendor to develop integrated processes for efficient service delivery, ask for feedback on their own performance, and in the case of a project, have clear deliverables for each milestone of the project.

Consider these questions as they relate to your government:

- *Does our IT staff have the skills to manage complex contract negotiations with vendors?*
- *Does our management use clearly developed outsourcing contracts?*
- *Does our IT staff have the correct technical skills to adequately support our complex technology?*

13

Quality Management Systems

MUCH LIKE THE quality movement that manufacturing went through in the 1980's to improve efficiency and lower costs, local governments are facing the same type of changes in how services are delivered.

Quality culture is a particular organizational orientation toward a set of values, principles, and definitions related to quality. A quality culture, as defined by the Malcolm Bridge National Quality Award, represents a way of working, a way of thinking, a personal commitment, and a lifestyle that is shared by members of an organization.

Quality can include attributes[12], such as:

- Continuous improvement in all activities and in all people
- Customer satisfaction for internal and external customers
- Efficient deployment of resources
- Employee, supplier, and customer development and recognition
- Environmental well-being
- Exemplary, visionary, and aggressive leadership
- Fast response time
- Full participation of employees, suppliers, and customers,

---

12 Malcolm Baldrige National Quality Award, 1995; Deming, 1986; Juran, 1992

- Life-long relationships with citizens
- Long-range perspectives
- Partnerships upstream, downstream, and across functions
- Prevention of error by designing in quality
- Process mapping and process improvement
- Attention to customer value
- Quantitative measurement and management-by-fact
- Root-cause analysis
- Shared values, vision, and culture
- Standard quality tools
- Top management sponsorship and involvement
- Waste reduction and cost containment

A criticism of using quality to enhance organizational effectiveness is that analysis of outcomes and effects is overlooked[13]. The U.S. General Accounting Office conducted a study of organizations that had implemented quality processes to investigate the relationships between quality processes and desirable outcomes. The 20 firms investigated all were finalists in the Malcolm Baldrige competition in 1988 and 1989. Each reported outcome data from the present back to the time they initially implemented quality processes.

The study concluded that firms implementing the quality process advocated by the Malcolm Baldrige program experienced continuous improvement in performance indicators and exceeded the industry averages in each of the four outcome categories. These categories included employee-related indicators, customer-related indicators, operational results, and financial results. Ultimately, the study validated the effectiveness of quality as an approach to improve organizational effectiveness.

Attempting to piece a framework around an existing set of processes will result in an ineffective system that experiences frequent failures.

---

13 Bowles, 1992; Crosby, 1992; Hammond, 1992; Crawford-Mason, 1992; McKoewn, 1992

Begin by designing your organization and processes, then finding a framework that helps to achieve your vision. Following consistent processes removes human error, reduces organizational risks, and reduces tangible and intangible costs.

MEANINGFUL METRICS

Always use data to make decisions, not just your gut feeling. Monitoring the metrics that provide the best insight into the welfare of your organization is key to understanding how well improvement efforts are really working. Not all metrics need to come from the same source – consider creative sources throughout the organization that can provide honest insight.

The Help Desk provides an opportunity to understand the effectiveness of your processes and IT. A good Help Desk manager can very well be more than just a trouble ticket administrator, and more of a quality systems analyst. For example, if the Help Desk decreases the average time to resolve an incident or decreases the number of reopened incidents. If there is a decrease in security incidents or the time to detect security incidents, the benefits of a Help Desk are obvious.

From our perspective, we suggest focusing on a framework such as ITIL, COBIT or ISPA that have well-defined metrics and prioritizing on key processes that are fundamental and align with the business goals.

Consider these questions as they relate to your government:

- *How do we know when IT is doing well?*
- *Are there any established metrics?*

14

Process Maturity & Why You Should Care

ULTIMATELY, THE GOAL is to define a performance baseline, and direct the IT organization on the path to self-improvement. *Sound impossible?* It's not. It just takes time, focus and funding. The Process Maturity program is designed to provide a methodical approach to improve operations, efficiency and effectiveness of an organization. Like any investment, it can be costly to embark on a Process Maturity program to improve overall functionality of your organization. But as the operations of the organization improve, you will begin to enjoy positive returns on your investment. This is a long-term, multi-year effort to improve your IT organization.

One common model for evaluating process maturity is the Capability Maturity Model (CMM), which is based on the assumption that organizations mature or improve their processes in stages based on solving process problems in a specific order. Developed by Watts Humphrey, a maturity model is a structured collection of elements that describe aspects of maturity in an organization. It can be used as a benchmark for comparison and as an aid to understanding.

Table 14.1 The five levels of process maturity
Maturity Level

1 **Initial**   Chaotic and unstable – the starting point for new processes. It is uncontrolled and reactive.

2 **Repeatable**   Process typically achieves repeatable outcomes.

3 **Defined**   Process is defined. There is a standard business process across the entire organization.

4 **Managed**   Process is successfully managed according to metrics defined in Level 3.

5 **Optimizing**   Process is improved with incremental and innovative technological changes.

CMM provides a framework to develop process maturity step-by-step from one level to the next level. Levels cannot be skipped in order to accelerate the process. Advancing process maturity can help IT managers gain better control of projects and daily operations, and increase their efficiency and effectiveness. It also helps managers understand the current state of their processes, the costs and benefits of pursuing process maturity, and the tools that are available to aid in transition from one level to another.

Within each maturity level, five Process Areas (PA) define the stages that organizations must go through to achieve the next Maturity Level. PAs provide management with detailed guidance through process maturity, which helps to improve the effectiveness and efficiency of their organizations. The five PAs are:

1. Goals
2. Commitment

3. Ability
4. Measurement
5. Verification

Begin by determining what the most critical processes are, how much you want to address, and establish metrics that track baseline performance to ensure you are enjoying positive results. Keep your expectations realistic, even achieving Level 2 or Level 3 is impressive and will show a marked improvement in your operations. Once the organization is stable, you can strive for 100% Process Maturity, but it's possible only if you have enough staff focused on advancing the organization.

FRAMEWORK OPTIONS FOR MANAGING IT PROCESSES

Frameworks frequently used to determine the effectiveness and manage IT in local government and other organizations include ITIL (Information Technology Infrastructure Library®), COBIT (Control Objectives for Information and Related Technology), MOF (Microsoft® Operations Framework), and the Information Systems Process Architecture (ISPA).

These are important, yet complex frameworks and it is suggested that any organization thinking of undertaking one seek the assistance of technical business professionals to provide guidance to you on the pros and cons of each IT framework and how well it would fit your unique environment. Think of them as quality management for IT. Here is a basic overview. First, ITIL is a set of concepts and practices for IT Service Management (ITSM), IT development and IT operations. It describes specific IT practices and offers checklists, tasks and procedures that any IT organization can tailor to its needs.

Next, COBIT is a framework for IT management created by the Information Systems Audit and Control Association (ISACA), and the IT Governance Institute (ITGI). It provides generally accepted measures, indicators, processes and best practices to maximize the benefits of IT, as well as develop appropriate IT governance and control. MOF delivers practical guidance for everyday IT practices and activities, helping users establish and implement reliable, cost-effective IT services.

Finally, the ISPA process framework created by the Society for Information Management (SIM) is a model of how a typical organization obtains and applies information systems and technology. The SIM process model: 1) defines strategically important IT processes in an overall framework; 2) communicates with IT stakeholders on the value, activities, and organization of IT; and 3) provides a basis for allocating IT resources that is compatible with activity-based costing.

SIM's ISPA process framework includes eight IT processes with specific metrics, and provides an example for organizing IT, determining core competencies, and identifying process owners.

SIM's ISPA Process Framework

Customer Relations

This process is used to develop and maintain working relationships with customers of IT products and services. Performance metrics focus on the business impact of IT, customer satisfaction, and product and service measurements, such as the accuracy and response time for solving problems or the number of viable IT projects identified.

Market IT

This process is used to ensure that customers want, need and buy the products and services offered. Sample metrics focus on the business value of IT, the return on investment (ROI) for IT, customer satisfaction, and product and service effectiveness.

Business and IT Alignment

This process is used to incorporate IT into strategic business change activities in a way that captures opportunities from current and emerging technologies, promotes process innovation leadership using IT, and uses proven change management techniques. Sample metrics focus on the business value of IT, the value of projects approved by the strategic business unit, and improvements to business processes.

Enterprise Architecture Management

This process is used to provide a framework for delivering consistent products and services. Sample metrics focus on IT architecture design and implementation, the number of viable IT projects identified, how service chargebacks align with customer views of services, and the degree of technology standardization.

Products and Services Development and Deployment

This process is used to acquire, develop, deliver, and implement new information services for the organization. Sample metrics might include the percent of projects on-time and with the desired functionality, projects completed within budget, customer satisfaction, and the level of technology usage in conducting core business processes.

Products and Services Delivery and Support

This process is used to ensure that the products and services are deployed in the most effective and efficient manner. Metrics can focus on customer satisfaction survey ratings, increased demand for IT information, adequacy of equipment and facilities, availability and accessibility of data, number of problems received and requests satisfied, and the time required to recover data.

IT Organization Plan

This process is used to shape and support business unit strategies; establish strategy and vision for long-term IT use; develop tactical plans and development and infrastructure resources over a 12 to 18 month period; and design key processes within the IT organization. Sample metrics include employee satisfaction with the IT vision and knowledge of technology plans.

IT Organization Business Management
This process is used to manage the processes within IT that deal with the health and state of the IT organization, its employees and vendors. Sample metrics include an employee satisfaction and commitment index, team efficiency and effectiveness measures, product and service measurements, and an index of employee skills.

As a local government manager, it is important to identify the key metrics that illustrate performance improvements in significant processes and document them. Before tackling a framework, like ITIL, COBIT or ISPA, identify your Process Maturity Level. Once identified, create a plan that shows the baseline performance and continually tracks improvements.

WHERE TO BEGIN

First, an organization needs to focus on improving fundamental processes, such as the Help Desk, change management, the systems administration, security administration, and continuity management. These will give you the greatest return on your time investment, and affect those processes performed the most by staff in your IT organization – which means a greater need for consistent performance.

Consider these questions as they relate to your government:

- *Does our IT department have clearly documented policies and procedures?*
- *Are the procedures followed?*
- *Who is responsible for enforcing the policies? User management or IT management?*

15

IT Projects Value-Risk Measures

N ow THAT WE have detailed the steps required to assess, define and
build an effective IT organization, it's important to understand how
to determine the value and risks of IT projects to the organization.

Value is a measure of the potential reward to the organization for
having a project completed. The organization's view of value is measured based on agreed upon weighted criteria that the organization sees
as important for all projects. Value may consider objectives such as:

- Improves service to citizens/residents/customers
- Causes measurable cost savings for local government
- Improves efficiency across several departments (e.g., reducing
  manual, redundant processes)
- Improves availability of information for proactive decision-making
- Updates hardware/software
- Improves the safety/security of local government information assets
- Satisfies requirements imposed by another governmental body
- Automates critical local government functions

The value to the local government must be broad in order to provide a
return to the majority of its stakeholders (e.g., individuals, groups, public

and private organizations). According to Anthony Cresswell from the Center for Technology in Government,[14] public value is best represented by six areas that governments can provide a positive result to stakeholders:

- **Financial** impact on income, asset values, liabilities, entitlements, and other wealth.
- **Political** impact on the ability to influence government actions or policy, or to participate in public affairs as a citizen or official.
- **Social** impact on family or community relationships, opportunity, status or identity.
- **Strategic** impact on economic or political advantage, or opportunities for future gain.
- **Ideological** impact on beliefs – moral or ethical – or positions.
- **Stewardship** impact on the public's view of government officials as faithful stewards in terms of public trust, integrity and credibility.

Risk is a measure of the threat assumed by the organization for launching a project (e.g., risk to the business, risk to the other departments for shifting resources to this project, risk of potential project failure). The organization's view of risk is measured based on agreed upon weighted criteria that the organization sees as important for all projects.

Risk considerations include:

- Financial risks (e.g., grant funding, cost of equipment)
- Technical, quality or performance risks (e.g., unproven or cutting-edge technology, or as-yet unproven integration of technologies)

---

14   "Return on Investment in Information Technology: A Guide to Managers," Anthony M. Cresswell, Center for Technology in Government, 2004.

- Project management risks (e.g., single resource/staff availability, scheduling)
- Organizational risks (e.g., impact core local government functions)
- External risks (e.g., business continuity disruption due to disaster, inability to locate specialized resources due to availability or cost)

These measurements are calculated in relative terms to each other. It is important that the organization have a consistent method for measuring the relative risk and value of projects under evaluation.

How the performance of IT is measured is a reflection of the role of IT in the organization. If IT is expected to simply maintain computers, the network and servers, it will remain a tactical cost center with no effect on the strategic direction of the organization. Performance is measured by simple metrics such as uptime, line-item budget compliance, SLAs and headcount. In this case, IT's full potential will never be realized in your organization.

When IT is a strategic contributor to the organization, performance is measured by new capabilities, process breakthroughs, technology innovations, and business-driven reports that show increasing value and less risk to government operations. Presenting recommendations for a technology investment requires a justification that relates it to improved efficiency and/or the ability to service citizens; but it's also important to explain how the investment affirms the technology architecture standards, simplifies business operations, and advances business objectives.

When creating an IT strategy, begin by defining senior management's tolerance for risk and the value expected of IT. Do a little government IT "soul searching" to understand the IT achievements that made the most impact in the past – both positive and negative. This analytical process has the added benefit of opening lines of communication between IT management and senior management. Once open, keep the lines of communication open.

Consider these questions as they relate to your government:

- *Is there a clear understanding of the value expected from each IT project?*
- *What are the potential risks of engaging in a new IT project?*
- *Does senior management have a high or low tolerance to risk?*
- *Does IT effectively communicate the risks when considering an IT project?*
- *Do we have the resources necessary to address the risks?*

16

Which Project First?

G OVERNMENTAL ORGANIZATIONS, IN general, are conservative in their investments and have exceptionally low risk tolerance. Project risk must also be viewed within the same framework. Traditionally, projects are evaluated one at a time. Higher risk projects are automatically eliminated – even projects with a potentially high value to the organization. This results in an inefficient use of resources as organizations tend to choose low-risk, low-value projects.

For example, using the traditional approach, an organization is considering three projects: (A) upgrading the fuel tracking system; (B) upgrading the city's financial system; and (C) creating a backup/failover data center. Each project is evaluated separately, and Project A is selected because it is low-cost and low-risk. Project B is rejected because it is high-cost and high-risk, despite the fact that the existing financial system does not meet users' needs and is obsolete. Project C is considered because it is low-risk, but is delayed indefinitely due to the cost.

In this case, the new fuel system is upgraded the following year, but the data from the system must be printed out and then re-entered into the existing financial system because the interface to the obsolete financial system was too costly. The financial system crashes regularly because the backup/recovery center was delayed. One of the crashes caused four days of lost work, and several days of lost data had to be re-entered.

The single project risk review process is inefficient and limited in its scope. Since technology projects tend to have higher risk profiles than other projects, organizations cannot succeed if they do not accept a certain level of risk. New methods have to be considered; portfolio project management is quickly becoming a best practice.

PORTFOLIO MANAGEMENT APPROACH

Portfolio management involves managing a collection of projects based on their overall value and risk profiles. In the end, the goal is to have a project portfolio that achieves and maintains the target value-to-risk profile. No two projects should have the same value-risk profile. By offsetting higher risk projects with lower risk projects, and lower value projects with higher value projects, the entire portfolio reflects the target cost-risk-value profile. So, the objective is not to eliminate risk, but to balance and manage the amount of risk taken.

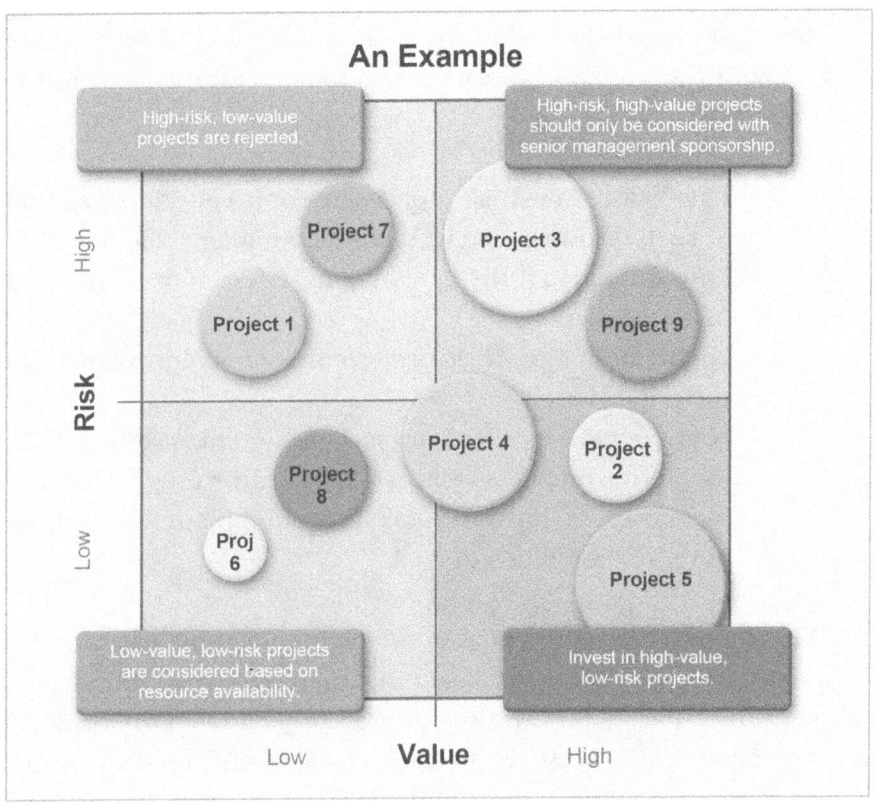

Figure 16-1 Value-to-risk comparison.

Each project is plotted against other proposed projects, as is shown in the diagram. Projects are evaluated on:

- Investment/cost to the organization. Plotted through the size of the bubble, where the higher cost projects are depicted with a larger bubble.
- Interdependencies, such as a project requiring streaming video for training and requires a project to increase the network bandwidth in the organization, are done first.

- Using this methodology, the projects are plotted within one of the four quadrants as shown in the Figure 16.1. Depending on where the projects fall within the four quadrants they can be prioritized as follows:

  — **Low-Value, Low-Risk** projects are only considered as filler to keep resources engaged between higher value projects.
  — **Low-Value, High-Risk** projects are rejected as unworthy of investment.
  — **High-Value, Low-Risk** projects are good investments for the organization.
  — **High-Value, High-Risk** projects are good investments for local government, as long as there is direct senior management sponsorship and a risk mitigation plan. Relatively few of these should be pursued.

The nine projects represented in the Figure 16.1 show the prospective projects being evaluated. Assuming that resources (i.e., money, staffing) are available, it is certain that projects #2 and #5 will be added to the portfolio because they offer a high-value and low-risk profile. Equally certain is that projects #1 and #7 will be rejected, because they represent the least favored profile, low-value and high-risk.

Once the project portfolio is approved, a timeline and investment schedule for the project portfolio is developed as part of the IT plan.

The challenge for most organizations is to know what to do next. Each of these projects has staff lobbying for the project, as well as the money to do it. If there is an unwillingness to assume much risk and no formal process for prioritizing projects, most organizations will opt for doing projects #6 and #8 because they cost less.

The decision between projects #3, #4 and #9 require detailed discussions of what went into the value and risk profiles. Special consideration should be given to projects whose value extends beyond the project, such as:

- Examine interdependencies between projects
- Isolate risk from other projects (e.g., deploying a wireless WAN that will be used by projects in the future)
- Funded from alternative sources (e.g., grants or Enterprise Funds)
- Enable organizational learning with new technologies or service approaches (e.g., deploying virtual servers) that can be leveraged throughout the organization in the future
- Extend the implementation timeline over a longer period with more frequent check-ins to evaluate project status

Let's look at the three projects we were considering earlier: (A) a fuel tracking system; (B) a financial system; and (C) a backup/failover center. In this example, the projects are being evaluated on both their value and their risk. As part of the risk evaluation, dependencies, such as the risk of the financial system failing and the lack of a backup center, would also be considered.

Based on this portfolio view example, the IT governance committee decides to proceed with the backup/failover center first, followed by the financial system at a later time when financial resources are available. They authorize the IT manager to use the fuel tracking system project as a filler project when the IT department's resources are available, but after the data center project is completed.

PUTTING THE PORTFOLIO TOGETHER

The decision about which projects will be done and when, and which ones will not, can be extremely divisive. While input should be sought from the broader organization into these critical decisions, ultimately these are executive decisions that should not be delegated.

It is easy for organizations to leave these decisions in the hands of IT. The rationale is that IT has the technical knowledge needed, but most organizations don't consider that IT lacks the business knowledge necessary to make informed prioritization decisions for the organization.

The best practice is to rely upon a group of senior managers, who form an IT Governance Committee and regularly review project plans and status reports.

Once a year, they will prepare for budgeting by:

- Defining strategic technology priorities for the overall organization
- Validating and/or updating the IT strategic plan
- Identifying, prioritizing and validating technical projects for the organization
- Reviewing recommendations for strategic directional changes

These important decisions are made with input and recommendations from the Project Management Office (PMO), a virtual organization used in many larger local governments that is comprised of customers, business analysts, project managers and other technical staff with a tactical, project execution focus.

MANAGING THE PORTFOLIO

IT organizations with the highest level of project performance have professionalized project management and project portfolio management through a PMO. These organizations recognize the need to hire trained project management professionals, standardize project management methodologies and processes, and monitor and report on the performance of projects. Learning from each project ensures that successful project execution is not person-dependent.

Whether you are in a smaller or larger local government, professional project management is one of the single most important factors in determining repeatable IT project success. The project manager provides the expertise and guidance on project plans, identifies challenges, creates risk avoidance plans, and makes project-related decisions that impact schedule, budget or project measurements. The project manager remains focused on the project as it relates to the needs of the departments and the constraints of IT, but they do not determine strategy, policy or protocols.

Business analysts gather, analyze and report on the needs of assigned departments. With knowledge of formal business and functional requirements, business analysts help to identify and select appropriate solutions. Additional analyses will determine the value and risk of projects to the organization within the adopted framework, including the impact of adding projects to the portfolio.

Whether you use a formal PMO or informal project evaluation process, your project managers must develop the project plan and submit it for evaluation. This includes a project charter, project schedule, budget, staffing needs, other resources and risk mitigation plan. These roles and their relationship to the PMO are represented in the diagram.

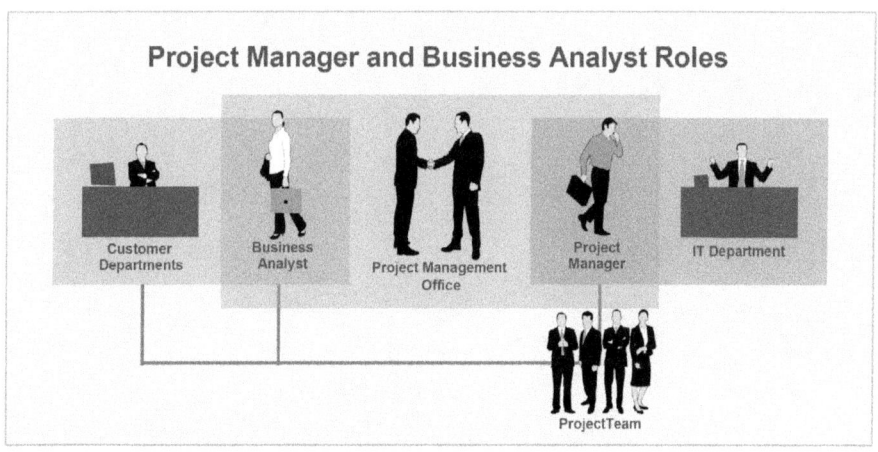

Figure 16-2 Project manager and business analyst roles

Once the PMO has approved a project, the scope of the project is provided to the IT Governance Committee for review. The work of the PMO may be formal or informal, depending upon the size and needs of your organization. Regardless of size, it is important to lay the groundwork for a successful project.

Sophisticated tools are available to assist with the implementation of a PMO in IT organizations, but many of these tools were created for large organizations facing a wide variety of software development projects. As a result, they may be more complex than the potential value they would deliver to smaller government entities.

Consider these questions as they relate to your government:

- *Is there a structured methodology for evaluating the IT projects to select?*
- *Are projects selected by a committee, IT management, or senior management?*
- *Does IT have the structure and process to help define the project requirements?*

17

Implementing the IT Strategy

A s we have established, all IT projects should support the organization's strategic business plans. The goals of the IT strategic plan are intended to contribute to the success of one or more objectives identified in the organization's overall plan.

Successful completion of all projects translates into a successful IT strategic plan ensuring that the organization's objectives are achieved. The integration of the local government goals, IT goals and IT processes leads to the effective delivery of information through projects that support business requirements.

Planning is a top-down process. Top level goals are defined by smaller objectives and assigned to the appropriate department to fulfill. For customer-facing departments, departmental projects come from departmental goals, which in turn stem from the departmental strategic plan. These plans are designed to achieve the objectives specified in the city's strategic plan.

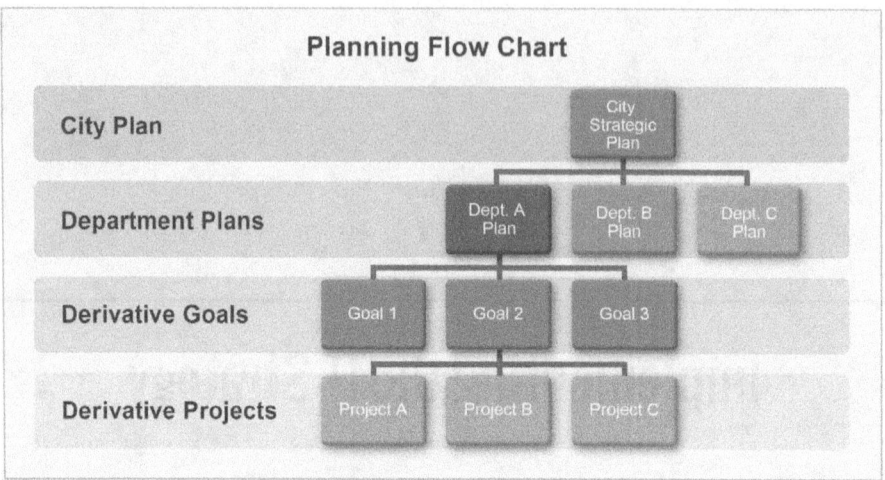

Figure 17-1 Planning flow chart

Departmental projects come in two basic forms: 1) improving customer support and/or customer service, (e.g., remote meter reading, centralized call center, streamlining applicant taking process); and 2) improving operating efficiency by providing infrastructure, (e.g., implementing purchasing cards, streamlining an approval process). In both situations, IT can play a key role.

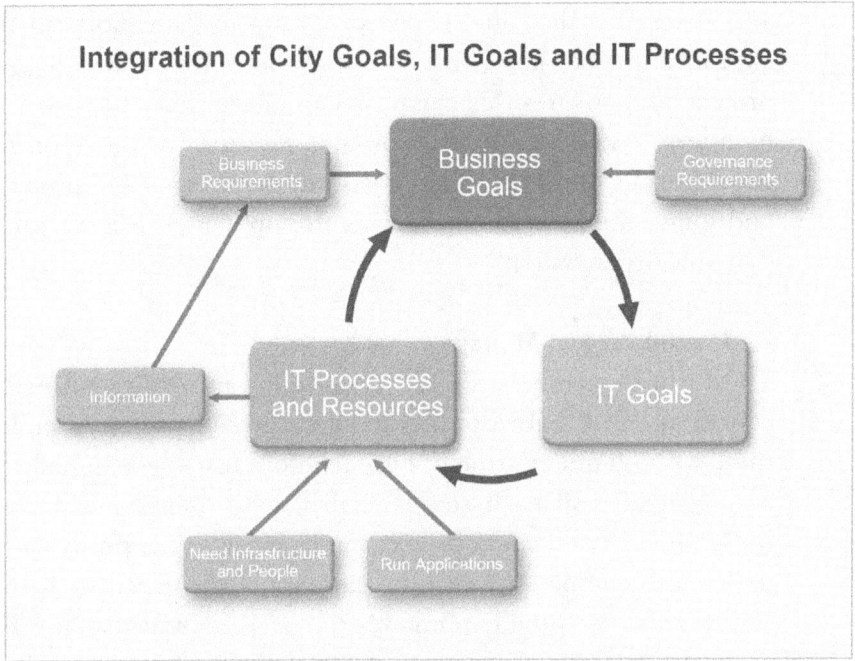

Figure 17-2 Integration of organizational goals, IT goals and IT processes

GUIDELINES FOR IT PROJECT LAUNCH

The IT Strategic Plan is heavily influenced by the direction of each department. Since IT cannot require each department to formalize a departmental plan, we recommend establishing a baseline of requirements from each department, and soliciting ongoing input into the ongoing changes. Strategic efforts should be separated from tactical actions. Effective communication ensures that needs are met, issues are identified early, and a positive relationship is maintained between IT and its customers.

Here are a few guidelines for a successful IT project launch:

- **Executive Sponsor**
  It's important for the project to have an executive sponsor with the authority to push the project through approval gateways,

and evangelize the value of the programs to gain support. An executive sponsor has a business need that will be solved by the project, and ensures that the project manager has access to the high-level resources and decision-making capacity. The sponsor should understand the need, costs and benefits of the project, and guide the project manager as the project evolves within a dynamic organization.

- **Dedicated Project Manager**
  The local government should also have a project manager to coordinate internal resources for a successful project completion. Without one person accountable for ensuring action items are completed at each step, the project is doomed to linger unfinished. A dedicated project manager owns the project and drives it to completion with the support of the executive sponsor. It is also essential to empower the project manager with the authority to make decisions and direct staff to achieve project goals.

  Typically, complex IT projects involve many moving parts, of which the vendor is providing only one. Even if an external vendor provides a project manager, that individual should only focus on the deliverables of the vendor, not the local government project overall. The local government must provide their own project manager who is focused on their success and the success of the entire project.

- **Split Project Manager Responsibilities = No Project Manager**
  We've witnessed resource challenged organizations attempting to split project management responsibility between two or more people in an effort to reduce the impact of the project on their "real jobs." We have also seen shared responsibility between a business department and IT. Splitting project management

responsibilities will result in no one being accountable for the project to ensure it is completed.

- **Task Tracking Drags Projects Down**
  Another potential project trap is too many reports. In an effort to keep everyone updated on the progress, project managers become task trackers, spending their time maintaining data in project tracking systems (e.g., tracking hours, tasks completion). Typically, this is the result of insufficient project planning, or failing to involve end users in planning – especially those who supply resources.

- **Unlimited Project Scope**
  Most organizations cannot answer the basic question: *When will this technology project be done?* In this situation, project objectives may not be clearly defined before the project is started. Many organizations skip formally defining the project objectives because of an overzealous project sponsor or the poor assumption that everyone understands what is needed.

  For projects without defined objectives, scope, budget and schedule, it is unclear whether a project is successful or is just simply completed. If a vendor has been contracted to perform work for this project without the added benefit of specific requirements, it is unclear whether the vendor has met the criteria for success in order to be paid.

Project Management

While most organizations throw subject matter experts into the role of project manager, most will flounder because they lack the specific skill sets needed. Project management is the discipline of planning, organizing, securing and managing resources to successfully meet project goals.

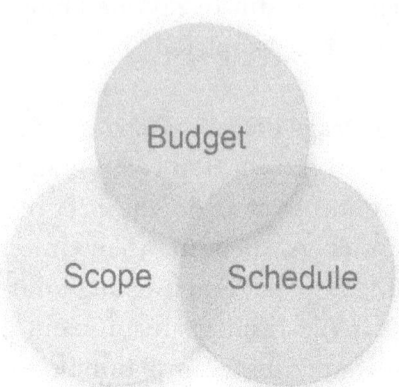

Figure 17-3 Triple constraints of project management

Successful project managers balance the "triple constraints" that include:

- Budget: Financial resources and other costs associated with the execution of the project.
- Scope: Requirements for the successful completion of the project.
- Schedule: Deadlines and milestones.

Often referred to as a three-legged stool, Figure 17.3 illustrates how adjusting any one of the constraints affects the other two. For example, if the budget for a project needs to be cut, then the scope and the schedule will both be affected.

Consider these questions as they relate to your government:

- *Does IT have experienced project managers?*
- *Does the business department have experienced project managers?*
- *Is a detailed project plan and scope of work developed at the kickoff of any major project?*

18

Where Do We Start?

FEW ORGANIZATIONS CAN go from chaos to high performing organization overnight. Start by collecting information about what needs attention to operate smoothly or more efficiently. We have found independent audits of organizations and their processes particularly beneficial. They typically deliver an unbiased perspective, and are able to benchmark against best practices and frameworks.

The top performing city/county governments find that assessing organizational readiness for a successful IT performance management system is essential. These organizations look for the involvement, commitment, and day-to-day support of enterprise senior managers. They also determine if they have adequate resources, including staff allocation, skills, time, tools, and use of consultants or technical assistance if needed.

One of our clients characterized a good performance management system as one that "has complete buy-in from top management, involves frontline employees in the system design, and ultimately enables frontline employees to understand what they do and why they are doing it."

Organizational readiness means making sure that existing planning and decision-making structures can accept and use performance results. As described earlier, performance measures are central to planning and alignment. These are essentially separate processes linked by performance measures.

The organization needs the capability to specify clear goals and objectives to set the focus and direction of IT performance, creating an IT performance improvement plan and reviewing it every few years. The IT organization has to understand the business of operational customers, and ensure that IT measures are consistent with business measures.

Lastly, organizational readiness means paying attention to organizational culture. *Is it receptive to data collection, measurement, and analysis and accountability for performance and decisions as part of an overall performance improvement system?* The organization should promote a philosophy that is positive toward performance management and measurement, and view it as a way to focus on quality and customer satisfaction. Organizations should be willing to assess organizational values, principles, and how they are working.

To recap the discussions in this book, here are reminders of the key points:

- Start with an assessment of where your IT organization is today.
- Pay close attention to metrics, such as critical success factors and key performance indicators, to gauge process and organizational inefficiencies.
- IT must be able to identify the need for strategic change, explain it to management, and deliver it.
- Organizational/structural changes should strengthen the organization's ability to deliver both strategic change and key infrastructure services.
- Document processes to establish IT as predictable and process-based.
- Define policies at the management level, so that IT is not responsible for both policy formulation and enforcement.
- Make enterprise IT purchase decisions by considering the interconnectedness of governmental systems and TCO, including

the resources required to support them over the life of the investment.

- The right tools will become mission critical to your business.
- Follow a rigorous selection process and involve staff.
- Define your requirements before looking at vendors.
- Encourage competition.
- Conduct a Cost-Benefit Analysis.
- Quantify the benefits.
- Improving the organization does not require a big investment all at once – do it over time and focus on only a few core processes.

IT can sometimes be a "dark hole" that senior managers do not understand. We hope that we have been able to clarify some of the reasons why IT performs as it does, and present a plan of action for improving the value that IT can deliver to your local government.

The first step requires action. It is our hope that this book has provided you with a little clear thinking to begin transforming your government.

GLOSSARY

3G – The third generation of mobile telecommunications technology based on a set of standards used for mobile devices and mobile telecommunications use services and networks that comply with the International Mobile Telecommunications-2000 (IMT-2000) specifications by the International Telecommunication Union.

4G LTE – A standard for wireless communication of high-speed data for mobile phones and data terminals.

Application software (apps) – A set of one or more programs designed to carry out operations for a specific application. Application software cannot run on itself but is dependent on system software to execute.

Backup – The process of copying and archiving computer data so it may be used to restore the original data after a data loss event.

Benchmarks – The act of running a computer program, a set of programs, or other operations, in order to assess the relative performance of an object, normally by running a number of standard tests and trials against it.

Bring Your Own Device (BYOD) – The policy of permitting employees to bring personally owned mobile devices (e.g., laptops, tablets, smart phones) to their workplace, and use those devices to access privileged company information and applications.

Capability Maturity Model (CMM) – A development model created to improve existing software development processes. The term "maturity" relates to the degree of formality and optimization of processes, from *ad hoc* practices, to formally defined steps, to managed result metrics, to active optimization of the processes.

Client/Server Computing – A distributed application structure that partitions tasks or workloads between servers and clients. Often clients and servers communicate over a computer network on separate hardware, but both client and server may reside in the same system.

Cloud Computing – The delivery of computing via a service rather than a product. Shared resources, software, and information are provided to computers and other devices as a utility over a network (typically the Internet). Clouds can be classified as public, private or hybrid.

Computer – A general purpose device that can be programmed to carry out a set of arithmetic or logical operations automatically.

Computer-Aided Dispatch (CAD) – The use of computer systems to assist in the creation, modification, analysis, or optimization of a design.

Control Objectives for Information and Related Technology (COBIT) – A framework created by ISACA for information technology (IT) management and IT governance. It is a supporting toolset that allows managers to bridge the gap between control requirements, technical issues and business risks.

Data – A set of values of qualitative or quantitative variables; pieces of data are individual pieces of information.

Digital Government – The digital interactions between a citizen and their government (C2G), between governments and government agencies (G2G), between government and citizens (G2C), between government and employees (G2E), and between government and businesses/commerce (G2B).

Disaster Recovery (DR) – A set of policies and procedures that enable the recovery or continuation of vital technology infrastructure and systems following a natural or human-induced disaster.

Downtime (Planned vs. Unplanned) – Time periods when computer systems are unavailable.

eGovernment – The digital interactions between a citizen and their government (C2G), between governments and government agencies (G2G), between government and citizens (G2C), between government and employees (G2E), and between government and businesses/commerce (G2B).

Enterprise Resource Planning (ERP) – A business management software—usually a suite of integrated applications—that a company can use to collect, store, manage and interpret data from many business activities.

Failover – Switching to a redundant or standby computer server, system, hardware component or network upon the failure or abnormal termination of the previously active application, server, system, hardware component, or network.

Federal Enterprise Architecture Framework (FEAF) – The enterprise architecture of a federal government that provides a common approach for the integration of strategic, business and technology management as part of organization design and performance improvement.

G2B (Government-to-Business) – The online non-commercial interaction between local and central government and the commercial business sector, rather than private individuals (G2C), with the purpose of providing businesses information and advice on e-business "best practices."

G2C (Government-to-Citizens) – The communication link between a government and private individuals or residents.

G2G (Government-to-Government) – The online non-commercial interaction between Government organizations, departments, and authorities and other Government organizations, departments, and authorities.

Geographic Information Systems (GIS) – A computer system designed to capture, store, manipulate, analyze, manage, and present all types of spatial or geographical data.

Hardware – The physical parts or components of a computer such as the monitor, mouse, keyboard, computer data storage, hard drive disk (HDD), system unit (graphic cards, sound cards, memory, motherboard and chips).

Help Desk – A resource intended to provide the customer or end user with information and support related to a company's or institution's products and services.

Information Systems Audit and Control Association (ISACA) – An international professional association focused on IT Governance.

Information Technology (IT) – The application of computers and telecommunications equipment to store, retrieve, transmit and manipulate data, often in the context of a business or other enterprise.

Information Technology Infrastructure Library (ITIL) – A set of practices for IT service management (ITSM) that focuses on aligning IT services with the needs of business.

Infrastructure – The basic physical and organizational structure needed for the operation of a society or enterprise, or the services and facilities necessary for an economy to function.

Internet Protocol (IP) – The principal communications protocol in the Internet protocol suite for relaying datagrams across network boundaries. Its routing function enables inter-networking, and essentially establishes the Internet.

IT Governance Institute (ITGI) – A nonprofit, global membership association for IT and information systems professionals that offers original research on global practices and perceptions relative to governance of IT.

IT Service Management (ITSM) – The implementation and management of quality information technology services.

Just in Time (JIT) – A production strategy that strives to improve a business' return on investment by reducing in-process inventory and associated carrying costs.

Process Areas (PA) – The goals required to improve a software process.

Leadership – A process of social influence in which one person can enlist the aid and support of others in the accomplishment of a common task.

Mainframe – Computers used primarily by corporate and governmental organizations for critical applications, bulk data processing such as census, industry and consumer statistics, enterprise resource planning and transaction processing.

Microsoft Operations Framework (MOF) – A series of guides aimed at helping information technology (IT) professionals establish and implement reliable, cost-effective services.

Mobility – Human–computer interaction by which a computer is expected to be transported during normal usage.

Multi-tenant – A principle in software architecture where a single instance of the software runs on a server, serving multiple client-organizations (tenants).

Network – A telecommunications network that allows computers to exchange data.

Operating System (OS) – Software that manages computer hardware and software resources and provides common services for computer programs.

Outsourcing – Contracting out of a business process to a third-party.

Process – A collection of related, structured activities or tasks that produce a specific service or product (serve a particular goal) for a particular customer or customers.

Process Maturity – A methodical approach to improve operations, efficiency and effectiveness of an organization.

Project Management Office (PMO) – A group or department within a business, agency or enterprise that defines and maintains standards for project management within the organization.

Real-Time Data – Information that is delivered immediately after collection

Records Management Systems (RMS) – The professional practice or discipline of controlling and governing what are considered to be the most important records of an organization throughout the records lifecycle, which includes from the time such records are conceived through to their eventual disposal.

Return on Investment (ROI) – The concept of an investment of some resource yielding a benefit to the investor.

Scalability – The ability of a system, network, or process to handle a growing amount of work in a capable manner or its ability to be enlarged to accommodate that growth.

Statement of Work (SOW) – A formal document that captures and defines the work activities, deliverables, and timeline a vendor must execute in performance of specified work for a client.

Server – A running instance of an application (software) capable of accepting requests from the client and responds accordingly.

Service-Level Agreement (SLA) – A part of a service contract where a service is formally defined.

Smartphone – A mobile phone with more advanced computing capability and connectivity than basic feature phones.

Social Media – The social interaction among people in which they create, share or exchange information and ideas in virtual communities and networks.

Society for Information Management (SIM) – A professional organization of over 4,000 senior IT executives, Chief Information Officers, prominent academicians, selected consultants, and other IT thought leaders built on the foundation of local chapters, who share and enhance their intellectual capital for the benefit of its members and their organizations.

Software – Any set of machine-readable instructions that directs a computer's processor to perform specific operations.

Strategy – A high level plan to achieve one or more goals under conditions of uncertainty.

Technology – The collection of tools, including machinery, modifications, arrangements and procedures used by humans.

The Open Group Architecture Framework (TOGAF) – An enterprise architecture framework for designing, planning, implementing, and governing enterprise information technology architecture.

Total Cost of Ownership (TCO) – A financial estimate intended to help buyers and owners determine the direct and indirect costs of a product or system.

Users – The people who use a computer or network service.

Virtual Machines (VM) – An software copy of a particular computer system.

Virtualization – Creating a virtual (rather than actual) version of something, including but not limited to a virtual computer hardware platform, operating system (OS), storage device, or computer network resources.

Wide Area Network (WAN) – A network that covers a broad area (i.e., any telecommunications network that links across metropolitan, regional, national or international boundaries) using leased telecommunication lines.

Workstation Clients – A workstation on a network that gains access to central data files, programs, and peripheral devices through a server.

ABOUT THE AUTHORS

Ernest Pages

As a founder and a partner at Sciens LLC, Management Consulting, Ernest Pages is an internationally recognized expert with over 25 years' experience in technology management, planning and design.

He has advised private and public sector CIO's and CEO's on the strategic use of technology for operations improvement. He balances technical depth with business savvy to help create effective implementations. He has successfully assisted senior management to converge on the technology vision, and has led the technical teams to effectively deploy the vision.

Tackling complex IT environments is one of Pages' strengths. In the early 90's, he lead a World Bank/Deloitte Touche (Deloitte) technical team to assist the Bolivian government with the privatization of their telecommunications sector. CitiBank also benefited from Pages' knowledge of utilizing IT to improve business operations when he managed a successful deployment of their global internetwork. He also worked with Gartner/Datapro to assist Federal Agencies in communications systems planning.

Today, Pages brings his experience and expertise to local governments – both city and county – to improve the efficiency and effectiveness of their operations, optimize their processes, and better leverage the technologies available. The Sciens methodology delivers field-proven, structured, replicable and scalable processes that can help to align government operations with the needs of the community.

He has earned extensive accreditations to ensure his clients benefit from his well-rounded knowledge. He is a Microsoft® Certified Systems Engineer (MCSE), a certified Information Systems Auditor (CISA), as well as certified in the Information Technology Infrastructure Library (ITIL), and in the Governance of Enterprise IT (CGEIT).

Pages earned a Bachelor of Science in Mechanical Engineering (BSME) from Florida Atlantic University, as well as a Master of Business Administration (MBA) and a Master of Science in Industrial Engineering (MSIE) from the University of Miami.

Stephen Gousie

As a co-founder and a partner at Sciens LLC, Management Consulting, Stephen Gousie is a nationally recognized expert in project management, business process analysis and reengineering, and technology acquisition. Gousie has worked with clients to create visionary strategic plans that are practical solutions respecting fiscal limits. His approach helps to improve processes and streamline the organization to eliminate inefficiencies.

Leading hundreds of projects with teams of all sizes in both the public and private sectors, he has managed projects in strategic planning and integrated systems definition and acquisition. His portfolio includes Enterprise Resource Planning, GIS/Land Management and Public Safety Systems, and their integration.

He is well-versed on quality management systems. He has conducted numerous detailed reviews of IT organizations using COBIT and ITIL best practices. As a result of his assessments, he has developed new organizational structures, governance mechanisms and technology direction.

With more than 20 years' experience driving strategic programs, Gousie has led teams at companies including NEC, Niteo Partners, Zefer Consulting, Information Mapping and the U.S. Customs Service. His knowledge of the public sector environment and of quality systems and technology help his clients improve their operations to achieve their vision.

Gousie is a certified Project Management Professional (PMP Certification #1324565) and Process Design Engineer (CPDE), as well as EXIN Certified in Information Technology Infrastructure Library.i Gousie earned a Bachelor of Arts (BA) in Economics from The George Washington University, and a Master of Science in Management (MSM) from Lesley University.

BIBLIOGRAPHY

IT Savvy: What Top Executives Must Know to Go from Pain to Gain by Peter Weill and Jeanne W. Ross. Harvard Business Press, 2009.

Information Technology Process Institute

Allen, Paul with Sam Higgins, Paul McRae and Hermann Schlamann, *Service Orientation: Winning Strategies and Best Practices*, 2006.

Erl, Thomas, *SOA: Principles of Service Design*, Prentice-Hall, 2007.

Erl, Thomas, *Service-Oriented Architecture: Concepts, Technology and Design*, Prentice-Hall, 2005

Fowler, Martin, David Rice, Matthew Foemmel, Edward Hieatt, Robert Mee, and Randy Stafford, *Patterns of Enterprise Application Architecture*, Addison-Wesley, 2002.

Hay, David C., *Requirements Analysis: From Business Views to Architecture*, Prentice-Hall, 2003. (Essentially a perspective on the Zachman Framework.)

Hohman, Luke, *Beyond Software Architecture: Creating and Sustaining Winning Solutions*, by Addison-Wesley, 2003.

Marks, Eric A. and Michael Bell, *Service-Oriented Architecture (SOA): A Planning and Implementation Guide for Business and Technology*, Wiley, 2006.

O'Rourke, Carol, Neal Fishman, and Warren Selkow, *Enterprise Architecture Using the Zachman Framework*, by Course Technology, 2003.

Perks, Col, and Tony Beveridge, *Guide to Enterprise IT Architecture.* Springer-Verlag. New York, 2003.

Trademarks

ITIL and *IT Infrastructure Library* are registered trademarks of the United Kingdom's Office of Government Commerce (OGC).

www.ingramcontent.com/pod-product-compliance
Lightning Source LLC
Chambersburg PA
CBHW051920170526
45168CB00001B/473